CENTER FOR THE STUDY OF POPULATION
FLORIDA STATE UNIVERSITY
TALLAHASSEE, FLORIDA 32306

THE BABY BUST

A GENERATION
COMES OF AGE

AMERICAN
DEMOGRAPHICS BOOKS.

A Division of American Demographics, Inc.
127 West State Street, Ithaca, NY 14850
Telephone: 607-273-6343

Executive Editor: Diane Crispell
Associate Editor: Shannon Dortch
Associate Publisher: James Madden
Assistant Editor: Sarah Sirlin

Paper back: ISBN 0-936889-21-7
Hard cover: ISBN 0-936889-20-9
Library of Congress Catalog Number 93-71267

Cataloging In Publication Data
Dunn, William, 1946–
The baby bust: a generation comes of age

Book Design and Composition: Stephen Masiclat
Cover Design: Rebecca Wilson

The Baby Bust:
A Generation Comes of Age

William Dunn

For Krisha,

Who convinced me that I did have books to write, encouraged me to write them, and lovingly supported me when I wanted to quit. Thank you. Once again, you were right.

• TABLE OF CONTENTS

PART I: THAT WAS THEN

Births plummet, catching experts and practically
everybody else off guard. And a new generation quietly rises.

Here's why Levittown is the quintessential boomer
artifact, and what it tells us about busters.

Home alone and scarce in the classroom,
baby busters are developing their own tastes and tendencies.

Busters shop early and often, usually at the mall.
They're ravenous consumers, but smart and demanding buyers.
They've had plenty of experience.

PART II: THIS IS NOW

Baby busters are the first generation to grow up with
computers, using them at home, school, and on the job.
Unintimidated by technology, they don't see what
all the fuss is about.

The baby busters are aggressively recruited by
universities. A higher proportion of them are going to
college than did baby boomers. Busters are also sticking
around campus longer—much longer.

PART III: AND THAT'S THE WAY IT'S GOING TO BE

APPENDICES

Acknowledgments

This book is based on extensive, albeit informal field observations, casual conversations, as well as formal interviews and experiments with baby busters. Some involved my relatives, young cousins, nieces, and nephews. In fact, these teens and young adults are the ones who first gave me the idea for this book, because they were so different from the mass-media caricature of the baby bust as a "lost generation."

Making allowances for my own bias, they were, objectively speaking, bright and informed, realistic, talkative, and cautiously confident, demonstrating the appropriate balance of doubt and concerns. While each had his or her individual interests and personalities, all were to varying degrees outgoing, active, and likable. There was little of the defeatism, confusion, and whining that the media forever trumpet.

Starting with my small circle of relatives and friends and going on to meet and talk to many other busters across the country, I've found busters to be unfairly maligned when they're not being needlessly overlooked. But take the time to get to know them and you will discover—as I did—that they're a surprisingly diverse and interesting generation, with promise, problems, and a lot to say. They were most cooperative and eager to be heard. They made this task educational and challenging, as well as fun.

I also want to acknowledge the contributions of Lionel Linder, a wonderful friend and the finest editor I ever had. I probably wouldn't have written this or my previous demographics book had I not had the good fortune to have Lionel Linder as my editor at the *Detroit News* many years ago. He taught me much of what I know about demographics and how to make it understandable and interesting to the reader. He was always encouraging and helpful, for which I'm thankful.

In his four decades in the newspaper business, he was a top editor at the *Albuquerque Tribune*, the *Chicago Daily News*, the *National Observer*, the *Detroit News*, and, finally, editor-in-chief of the *Memphis Commercial Appeal.* He was fascinated by trends of all types and encouraged his reporters to dig below the surface to find out the causes and repercussions, and how they might influence the future.

In an era when journalism has become increasingly politicized and superficial, Lionel Linder demanded his reporters do it the right way. He taught his reporters and editors to be thorough and fair, to cover all the angles, write clearly and with style, and always respect the reader. He never dodged tough, sensitive stories. But he also required that his reporters present the possible solutions along with the problems.

Unfortunately, Lionel won't be reading this book. He was killed in a tragic car accident late last year. His death was a true loss to journalism. But his contribution was significant and continues, for the many hundreds of reporters he groomed and encouraged over the years are writing today for top publications across the nation and doing it better for having had Lionel Linder as their mentor and friend.

Introduction

They've been called the "doofus generation," by the *Washington Post;* "the boomer's shadow" by the *Detroit News;* " the nowhere generation" by *Esquire Magazine;* and "twentynothings" by the *Asbury Park Press.* Words used to describe them have included: whiny, cynical, angry, perplexed, tuned out, timid, searching, vegged out—the latest lost generation. "They"—as if they were the feared aliens of the science fiction thriller "Them"—are the baby busters, 41 million Americans born between 1965 and 1976 plus the 3 million more in that age group who have immigrated here.

If I were a baby buster, I'd call up the local branch of the ACLU and file a class-action suit, alleging slander against a worthy generation. At the very least, I'd cancel my subscription to the various publications defaming 44 million individuals and consumers. That's more than the populations of three-quarters of the world's nations.

In 1993, busters are aged 17 to 28—a pretty important piece of the lifecycle. It's the time when young people traditionally enter the labor force, get married, start having children, buy homes, and have growing incomes, rising consumption, and increasing influence on the economy and culture.

They are over 17 percent of the population and would seem to be an attractive, enormous, and lucrative target for marketers of goods and services. Yet, they've been largely ignored by marketers, politicians, and trend trackers, probably because prior to the recent rash of dismissive buster coverage, the media ignored them, too. The media, marketers, and other institutions instead have obsessively focused their longing gaze on the massive baby-boom generation. In the brutal competition for boomer bucks, many busters succeeded in being stampeded.

The Buster's Burden

Busters are, indeed, an important generation, our future leaders, and well worth getting to know. But we know so little about them and so much about boomers. The incessant boomer coverage started three decades ago, with fawning cover stories in the newsweeklies, the *New York Times,* and on the nightly news. That was no coincidence: the editors and reporters of those stories were themselves the marveling parents of baby boomers.

By the early 1980s, boomers were succeeding their mothers and fathers—mostly their fathers—as senior reporters and editors at the elite media. Instead of writing about their children, they wrote about themselves, perpetuating and expanding the stereotypes and sweeping generalizations that obscured the diversity of this generation.

In 1980, *Fortune* magazine put its phrase-makers to work on a profile of the new breed of young professionals then entering the race around the fast-track and coined the term "yuppie," shorthand for young, upwardly mobile professional. Journalists and analysts pounced on the phrase. To many people, it became a synonym for college-educated boomers.

Terms like yuppies, buppies (black yuppies), nimbys (not in my backyard), dinks (dual income, no kids), and even boomers are the essential building blocks for headline writers, million-dollar anchors, and ink-stained wretches who rely on catchy phrases to pique the public's interest and quickly and simply convey complex information and images. Trends and information become oversimplified, though, and the rich details get lost in the broad brush-strokes.

Media Myths and Myopia

All but lost in the boomers' self-absorption and journalists' and marketers' blind chase after them is the smaller, yet still sizable and increasingly important baby-bust generation. As the media and others slowly and belatedly begin to pay grudging attention to baby busters, after two decades of ignoring them, I'm struck also by the routinely critical and superficial portrait—the "doofus" caricature—that's painted of an entire generation. The busters I know are much more interesting and varied than the media let on.

But images of the hapless busters are really not surprising when one considers who's doing the reporting—baby boomers. Boomers are just doing what adults have done throughout the history of mankind: criticizing and dismissing younger generations as unworthy successors who didn't endure the hard knocks that they vividly remember. Boomers forget that that's what their own parents did to them in the 1970s and 1980s.

One striking exception has been Bill Clinton, America's first baby-boom president. In his bid for the White House, Clinton actively wooed busters by appearing on the late-night "Arsenio Hall Show", and on MTV, the rock video network. Look where it helped land him: 1600 Pennsylvania Avenue.

Sure, Clinton aggressively pursued votes of boomers and seniors, too. But he was the first politician to consider busters seriously as part of the mix. It paid off. Of 17 million Americans aged 18 and 29 who voted, 44 percent pulled the lever for Clinton, 33 percent for George Bush, and 23 percent for Ross Perot. Only four years before, the majority in that same age group and the electorate generally had supported George Bush.

Setting political allegiances aside, the busters proved that they are very much plugged into the process, demanding to be heard and taken seriously even though most Americans haven't figured this out yet.

Let me now utter three heresies before proceeding to the heart of the matter.

One: I, an unwilling member of the baby-boom generation—unwilling because membership comes with distinct liabilities–find my generation overindulged, overrated, and overly covered by the media, even with a boomer in the White House.

Two: I find baby busters overindulged in some respects and not in others, but clearly underrated as a group, paid too little attention to, and definitely misunderstood.

Three: Media, marketers, educators, planners, and others persist in their boomer/buster delusions at their own peril.

With this book, I humbly attempt to correct all three problems. Herein:

- Boomers get close but brief scrutiny.
- Busters move center stage, into the spotlight, in their first starring role.
- Media, marketers, and planners, as well as the parents, spouses, and other loved ones of boomers—and especially busters–gain a better understanding and appreciation of these distinct, influential, and complex generations.

The book is divided into three main parts: That Was Then, This is Now, And That's the Way It's Gonna Be. At the end of each chapter in Parts II and III is a section titled "Buster Biz," in which we explore various marketing opportunities presented by busters.

In addition to comments and research from appropriate expert sources from the social sciences, economics, and education, there are also selections from the real experts—busters themselves. Throughout this narrative, you'll find their experiences and perceptive observations from the frontlines. In each chapter, they have their own buster bully pulpit, Vox Buster, from which to sound off.

Herewith, the first volley.

• VOX BUSTER •

"It's wonderful that somebody is finally going to say some-thing about us—hopefully not negative. Most recently I remember reading a story in Time *magazine about the 'twentysomethings.' It floored me to think that the establish-ment thinks that we're nobody, going nowhere ...*

"It's like, either in the classroom or the media, be it on the television or what you read, I've never felt like there's this overwhelming support or encouragement for what we could do. That sounds kind of big and out there. But I think it needs to be addressed."

—Lizabeth MacDonald, 23, Washington, D.C.

Right, you are, Lizabeth. And away we go.

William Dunn
Chevy Chase, Maryland
November 8, 1992

PART I

That Was Then

•

CHAPTER ONE

Buster Beginnings

Births plummet, catching experts and practically everybody else off-guard. And a new generation quietly rises.

As shoppers mobbed the stores during the Christmas season of 1964, 32 merchants in Centralia, Illinois, were busy with their own gift-giving. They were stockpiling toys, diapers, bibs, blankets, strollers, playpens, and other items for the annual Baby Derby, to give to the first baby born in the New Year.

The *Centralia Sentinel* had been sponsoring the Baby Derby since the Depression. The proud parents and unimpressed derby winner always made for a fun front-page story and picture on January 2, the day after the blessed event. But the schedule got goofed up in 1965 in Centralia. Things were mighty quiet in the maternity ward at St. Mary's Hospital on New Year's Day and a few days afterwards. In fact, the winner of the derby didn't arrive until January 5, 1965.

In the next day's edition, the local paper duly reported: "The *Sentinel's* Baby Derby king remained nameless today. Why? Because his parents, Mr. and Mrs. Tyrone (Tony) Shook, have decided the only name they had picked out earlier—Jennifer—just won't do." Two days later, under the headline "King Gets Name," the *Centralia Sentinel* informed its readers that the 1965 Baby Derby winner would henceforth be known as Barry Dale Shook. While his late arrival might have been a tip-off that a new trend was aborning, no one noticed at first. But baby Barry, today aged 28 and an electrical engineer in Peoria, has the distinction of being one of America's very first baby busters.

Marietta Broughton, a *Sentinel* editor who had worked on the Baby Derby for many years, vaguely recalls the late arrival of the first baby in 1965. "I thought it was a fluke. I didn't see a trend at all," she admits these many years later. Few people anywhere across America did, even though day by day, fewer babies were being born than the year before, and many fewer than just eight years earlier in 1957, the peak of America's baby boom.

Looking back through yellowed newspaper clips and microfilm, the newspaper's librarian Theresa Schaefer says: "I guess it takes longer to get a New Year's baby." Indeed, yes, Theresa. By the end of 1965, only 247 babies had been born in Centralia, compared with 309 the year before and 329 in 1959. Nationally, births dropped below 4 million in 1965 for the first time in 12 years. Births in Centralia, throughout Illinois, and across the nation kept falling year by year. People and institutions paid little attention, with a few exceptions.

THE ROLLER-COASTER TREND: BIRTHS FROM 1946 TO 1991

Annual births in millions

source: *National Center for Health Statistics*

One of the few to notice was Gerber Products, which has an obvious stake in birth trends. Gerber, headquartered in Fremont, Michigan, looked at the declining numbers and began diversifying in the late 1960s, into trucking, insurance, and children's furniture. Unlike most companies, it was getting birth data directly and regularly from the

3

government—the National Center for Health Statistics (NCHS). NCHS then was issuing twice-yearly reports on births, deaths, marriages, and divorces.

Gerber had been tracking birth trends since the 1930s, when its salesmen drove through neighborhoods counting diapers on clotheslines and used that information when calling on local grocers to boost their orders for Gerber baby food. But most other companies and institutions probably didn't know about the downturn in births. Few reporters, even in the business press, noted the steady decline or realized its potential repercussions. Why bother? The economy was still growing strong in the pre-inflationary late 1960s and unemployment was low.

The few who spotted the falling birth rate dismissed it as temporary, a postponement of marriage and parenthood due in large part to the Vietnam War. As frequently happens, the so-called experts misinterpreted what they saw. "Demographic projections are essential to an understanding of social issues and to the establishment of policies. They are often wrong," wrote William Alonso, professor of population policy at Harvard University, in *Demographic Change and the American Future.*

"During the Depression, when U.S. birth rates were falling, projections promised a leveling off and even a decline in the American population. They did not anticipate the baby boom. During the 1960s, conversely, projections conjured up visions of very rapid growth, with the population doubling within a half century. As fertility has declined, projections have declined as well, although more slowly, as though demographers were not quite believing what was happening: census projections continued to use as their 'middle' assumption a total fertility rate of 2.1 (the replacement level) long after the actual rate had been 15 percent lower for a number of years," according to Alonso.

One of the first to realize that this was no aberration but an important new trend was policy analyst George Grier, now senior associate at the Greater Washington Research Center. "Analyzing early 1970 census results ... we came across a startling set of facts," wrote Grier in a 1971 report titled *The Baby Bust.* "While America's young-adult population had increased at the fastest rate in recorded history during the 1960s, the national small-child population had actually declined by nearly one-sixth.

"We follow the news pretty carefully, but we had not heard of any such dramatic change in national fertility patterns. We simply recalled reading something to the effect that births had recently been declining somewhat, but that the trend was unlikely to continue." But Grier correctly cautioned: "The unprecedented nature of the recent population trends could mean that all of the 'rules of the game' regarding fertility and population growth have changed."

By 1973, births in the U.S. had dropped 27 percent—fully 1.1 million fewer babies than were born in the peak year of 1957. By then, people and businesses couldn't help but notice that something was going on, as repercussions of the decline became increasingly evident.

When Barry Shook was born in 1965, there were three maternity and baby shops in Centralia. In subsequent years, they saw their sales decline. One by one they went out of business, casualties of dropping births and competition from shopping malls.

• VOX BUSTER •

"I never really saw myself as a group. I never heard this name before—baby buster. I always just thought of us as the generation after the baby boomers—not really a name."

—Holly Woung, 24, Washington, D.C.

During the baby boom, working dads and homemaker mothers had on average 3.7 children, stretched over a decade or more. By the mid-1970s, the average couple had fewer than two children. Tyrone Shook, a banker, and his wife Carolyn had two children. The size of their family was dictated "probably by economics and lifestyle. I think our main concern was how many children we could educate and take care of," says Mrs. Shook, who juggled child-rearing and a job. "All of our friends have two, three at the most. And some just have one. We're the norm," adds Mrs. Shook, now 52.

5

Two babies per couple is just below what demographers call replacement level, the 2.1 children a couple must have to replace themselves (the extra 0.1 is to compensate for children who die before reaching the childbearing years themselves).

Barry Shook started to notice the impact of the baby bust in high school, where he played trombone and tuba in the marching band. "My freshman year, it started to drop off from years before when there were up around 180 to 200 in the band," recalls Shook, who grew up in the southwestern Illinois town of Salem. By the time he was a senior, the band was down to around 110 musicians. "We kept a pretty good balance of instruments. It's just that everything was smaller. And in the world of marching bands, smaller is not quite as loud and doesn't have the impact. So consequently, you're not quite as competitive."

Coaches in some schools in Illinois and other states hit by the baby bust found it increasingly hard to field enough players for sports like football, much less winners. Shook, who played football as well as trombone, remembers: "The teams did get progressively smaller as the classes graduated."

Graduating first in his high school class, the 1965 winner of the Centralia Baby Derby enrolled in the Rose-Hulman Institute of Technology in Terre Haute, Indiana. "My class in college was the smallest that had gone through in a long time ... As I went through college and got into the later years, you could see the recruiting department at the college start to really step up some programs and get the recruiting going, get students to try to call up prospective high school seniors, trying to keep the enrollment up."

Ready or not, here come the busters. "They're next," says Brad Edmondson, editor-in-chief of *American Demographics* magazine. "We don't have a substitute."

And the rest of us better get to know and understand them quickly, because they're all grown up already.

CHAPTER TWO

The Boomer Legacy

Why Levittown is the quintessential boomer artifact, and what it tells us about busters.

To understand the baby bust, one first must understand and appreciate baby boomers and the far-reaching impact of their numbers. Consider, for example, the story of the Martin family, a quintessential example of how the boom boomed.

Jo-Ann Martin Fink, a 46-year-old Long Island homemaker, is the first daughter of pioneers, and a bit of American history herself, though she laughs off the suggestion. But she and her family are also a key to understanding the baby bust. Without people like Jo-Ann Fink, the baby bust would have no meaning, for she is in the first wave of the post-World-War-II baby boom, which is forever casting its long shadow on the generation behind it. Fink was also one of the first babies born in Levittown, New York, the prototypical American suburb that sprouted up after World War II to house returning GIs and their brides.

On October 1, 1947, opening day, some 300 families moved into Levittown, built over what had been potato fields. Two weeks later, Joseph Martin, an Army vet who fought in the Battle of Corregidor, and his wife Beatrice moved out of her parents' house into their very own two-bedroom Cape Cod. Being on a corner lot, the house was a bit more expensive than others, a whopping $8,350. The Martins' monthly mortgage payment was $57. "The local newspaper took pictures of us when we went to purchase the house. And they called us pioneers," recalls Mrs. Martin. "It was quite an adventure."

What had been a farming community with only 450 people before World War II mushroomed in less than a decade to over 56,000 residents living in 17,447 homes, collectively known as Levittown for its builder William Levitt. It had 9 public swimming pools and 72 playing fields.

"You have to remember, these weren't 17- or 18-year-olds, first getting married," notes Joe Martin. "Everybody was in their 20s, because the war stopped a lot of people from getting married. Then when they did get married, they were ready to settle down. They knew they were going to have families; they knew they had responsibilities."

Beatrice and Joseph Martin's first child, Jo-Ann, was born in late 1947. The Martins added two more bedrooms to their Cape Cod. Two other children followed in 1950 and 1957. The home that the Martins bought for $8,350 and still live in is now valued at $150,000. Baby boomer Jo-Ann Fink is now herself the mother of baby busters. "They're going to bust me," she jokes.

The Postwar Baby Boom

Boomerwise, Levittown is a microcosm of America. While Levittown's boom began in the fall of 1947, America's baby boom began some nine months after V.E. Day and kicked into high gear nine months after V.J. Day. Marriages, which had predictably dropped off during the Depression and war years, jumped to 1.6 million in 1945— 161,000 more than the year before. In 1946, 2.3 million couples tied the knot—the most marriages the U.S. had ever had up to that point. The babies weren't far behind. Births reached 3.4 million in 1946 and kept climbing, breaking through 4 million by 1954 and peaking at 4.3 million in 1957. For 11 straight years, births topped 4 million. Not until 1965 did births drop below this number, signaling the end of the post-war baby boom. Between 1946 and 1964, some 75.9 million babies were born in America, and the country hasn't been the same since.

With immigration adding almost 2 million more to that age group, boomers altogether now represent over 30 percent of the U.S. resident population. As Gregory Spencer, an analyst at the Census Bureau, once advised *USA Today:* "Society's attention is wherever the heck the baby boom is going to be. Whatever concerns a third of the population will be a major concern to our society." Marketers have difficulty keeping up with demand.

The formula was simple: more marriages times 3.7 babies (average at the peak of the baby boom) equaled more consumers, ever-rising sales, more production jobs, and more spending. Many assumed the baby and economic booms would go on for decades, a logical counterpoint to the scarcity of the Depression and World War II.

It wasn't until the fall of 1951 that educators, planners, politicians, and others began glimpsing a few of the liabilities of the baby boom. Before then, boomers had been at home, in the loving embrace and protective custody of their homemaker mothers, and in the company of all the other children on the block—kid heaven. Then came September 1951, and America's school systems were swamped by a wave of boomer kids.

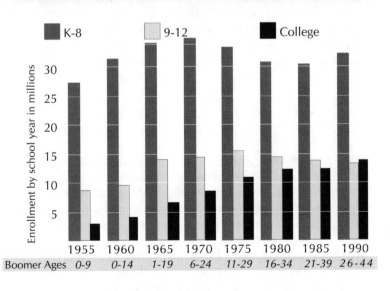

BABY-BOOM SCHOOL ENROLLMENT: K-12 & COLLEGE

K-8   9-12   College

Enrollment by school year in millions

30
25
20
15
10
5

	1955	1960	1965	1970	1975	1980	1985	1990
Boomer Ages	0-9	0-14	1-19	6-24	11-29	16-34	21-39	26-44

9

source: National Center for Education Statistics

This is an eyewitness account. I was there that first year in a kindergarten class at St. Rose of Lima School in Millburn, New Jersey. There were 57 children in one classroom, 114 eyes gazing upon one young, overwhelmed teacher. Some of us were forced to buddy-up at one desk, on one seat, which didn't leave much room for the guardian angels that the nuns said each of us had accompanying us every minute. A three-story addition was thrown onto St. Rose of Lima School, increasing classroom size by over one-third.

Down the block, a new public high school was built in what had been an empty field; the previous public high school was demoted to the junior high school. Then they had to put a state-of-the-art addition on the newly minted junior high.

It was the same across America, and the boomer flood only grew more intense. A *New York Times* article, dated September 21, 1987 said of Levittown's early days: "The community almost immediately needed a school district. 'In 1949 we had potato fields,' said Dr. Herman A. Sirois, Superintendent of the Levittown School District. In 1950 we had a school system. In 1952 we had 10,000 students."

Post-war America was growing, and its families were growing so fast, and so confidently, that they were growing out of their houses, schools, offices, and playgrounds. America embarked on a blind building and production spree. Construction was one of the fastest-growing industries of the 1950s. Roads, sewers, fire, and police protection—all the essential services that are now inscrutably known as "infrastructure"—expanded with the increasing demands of boomers and their parents. The taxes needed to pay for it all grew, too.

The Pig in the Python

Boomers have been described by demographers as the pig in the python. They can also be called the tidal wave forever crashing onto the beach that is American society. Society, its institutions, and citizens must forever stretch and be reconfigured to accommodate—willingly or not—the sheer size of the boomer generation.

What happened in grade schools in the early 1950s was only a taste of what was to come in high schools, colleges, the housing market, and the workplace. Despite all the media noise about the power, purity, and New-Age idealism of the trend-setting baby boomers, the boomers themselves were discovering a few real-world liabilities: never-ending competition for everything. When confident boomers applied to college after years of being told they were special and the smartest ever, many were rejected by their top choices, simply because so many others were applying to the same schools.

College diplomas were advertised as the ticket to success. But boomers began flooding the labor force in the late 1960s and through the 1970s. While the economy continued expanding, particularly during the Vietnam War, it had difficulty absorbing all the job-seeking baby boomers, many of whom were unpleasantly surprised at how long it took to land real jobs, unlike the make-work jobs they easily landed during their school years.

There were so many applicants, so many entry-level workers, all competing with one another, that the oversupply only served to drive down salaries and wages. And as boomers climbed the corporate ladder, the steps seemed steeper, not only because of the inherent competitiveness of upper-management jobs, but also because of the sheer numbers of capable boomer applicants.

While their parents are retiring in their early 60s and reaping the full benefit of Social Security, the boomers' large numbers are guaranteed to strain the system, forcing them to work longer. To borrow the quip about former liberals who became neo-conservatives in the 1970s and apply it to the aging boomers of the 1990s: They've been "mugged by reality."

Nevertheless, boomers, despite the obstacles they face, have always been and will remain a seductive target—or targets—for marketers of goods and services, who think it's easier and more profitable to hit a big target. Marketers are lured by visions of launching the next hula hoops, bongo boards, coonskin caps, blue jeans, 45-rpm records, Mustang convertibles, all driven into the marketing hall of fame by boomer consumers. The hopeful marketers conveniently forget mood rings, Nehru jackets, countless and now-forgotten one-hit rock stars, Gablinger's Beer, or innovative cars like the AMC Gremlin.

In 1993, boomers are, no doubt against their collective will, aged 29 to 47. The Pepsi Generation is now middle-aged. Marketers and media, as if in a herd, are trying to age right along with the boomers. As a result, growth industries include opticians, skin and hair care, health and fitness, recreation, home remodeling, financial planning, and nostalgia.

Many marketers are getting rich. But others struggle in the face of brutal and increasingly crowded competition for boomer bucks, while ignoring less competitive markets, such as the busters. Nowhere is that more evident than on the radio airwaves.

THE BABY BOOM IN THE LABOR FORCE

Distribution of the U.S. work force by age.

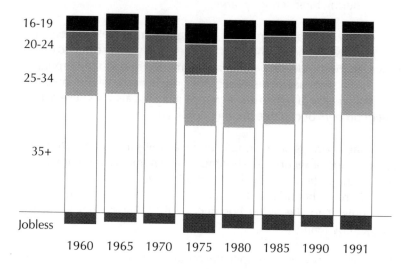

source: U.S. Bureau of Labor Statistics

"Generally, we find that baby busters are being ignored by radio.... They are not this big blob that people see as an easy target," says Robert Unmacht, editor of the radio industry trade publication *M Street Journal*. "Stations are throwing away their formats to go back and try to aim to the 25- to-54-year-old center. What you've got now are 70 to 75 percent of the radio stations chasing the baby boom and ignoring the rest of the population that's not in the baby-boom category." In other words, three-quarters of the radio stations are chasing one-third of the population.

Stations up and down the dial now feature golden oldies, classic rock, and country & western, all aimed at boomers. "You're hearing less top-40, contemporary-hit radio, which aims for an audience under 25," contends Unmacht. "I don't know of too many other businesses that are so crazy about attracting baby boomers that they are actually cutting their own throats."

• VOX BUSTER •

"I feel like I'm caught between generations. You've got this big baby-boom generation setting the trends and lifestyles. It seems like they're glorified, along with the sixties. In a way, I'm kind of tired of it. What about us? I think we've been overlooked. We're the future of America. We're the ones going into these entry-level positions and moving up the ladder, taking the place of those getting older. I guess we're kind of out of time and out of place. ... On the one hand, you've got Teenage Mutant Ninja Turtles; on the other, there's Depend Undergarments. Well, where are marketers targeting me?"

—Daniel Holland, 24, Pittsburgh, Pennsylvania

CHAPTER THREE

A New Tradition

Home alone and scarce in the classroom, baby busters are developing their own tastes and tendencies.

The pink slips came every year, like budding flowers, a sure sign of summer and school vacation. For many years, nobody took them seriously. School boards routinely laid off low-seniority teachers at the close of school, only to rehire them once the fall budget and enrollment firmed up.

"I had been pinkslipped once before," says Alexander Hardie, a veteran Michigan phys-ed teacher who was promptly rehired in the summer of 1979 by the South Redford school district. Then in the spring of 1980, at age 43 and after 20 years in teaching, Hardie was pinkslipped for real. "My principal, who was a very good friend of mine, gave me my pink slip. And he cried," Hardie vividly recalls. "The thing I remember is that it wasn't pink. I think it was yellow."

By the early 1980s, Hardie's wife, Eleanor, who taught in the neighboring Livonia school district, got bumped out of her position at the junior high level and wound up teaching elementary school, bouncing from one grade to another for several years.

14

Like many other teachers before and since, the Hardies were caught off guard. "When I graduated from college in 1960, the education field was wide open. There was no one getting laid off. School districts were very, very crowded. They were packed to the gills," Alexander notes.

It was the same across the country. During the 1950s and 1960s as the baby boom sent enrollment skyward, educators scrambled to hire enough teachers and throw up new classroom buildings to accommodate the bulge. But enrollment stopped growing by the early 1970s. What some mistook for a stabilization in births and enrollments was the precarious plateau before the plunge that caught many by surprise. As early as the mid-1970s, the South Redford school district began laying off teachers.

"Very few experts will tell you this [baby bust]was expected," Livonia superintendent George G. Garver told the _Detroit News_ in 1982. "In my opinion, the advent of the Pill and women's emancipation brought about a change in the birth rate that was so quick, it was impossible to anticipate. We got caught in the growth cycle and believed that it would continue forever."

Even Levittown, where enrollment jumped from a few hundred in 1947 to 19,000 by the mid-1970s, suffered an enrollment free-fall. People weren't moving out. In fact, they were still moving in. But the newcomers, as well as the young couples who had grown up in Levittown, were having smaller families. Smaller families meant fewer students to educate. By the fall of 1992, the Levittown student body totaled only 6,551.

In youth-obsessed California, where the population almost doubled from 1950 to 1970, to 20 million, many school districts saw their student bodies triple and quadruple. State elementary and secondary public school enrollment swelled 168 percent between 1950 and 1970, reaching 4.5 million. But by 1980, California's enrollment dropped to a 16-year low of 3.9 million. Across the U.S., elementary enrollment peaked in the fall of 1969, at 36.7 million students. High school enrollment topped out in the mid-1970s, at 15.7 million.

Why the Bust Happened

What no one could predict was that several forces would collide in the 1960s and 1970s to drive birth rates and family size down, and to shape the buster experience and outlook.

BUSTING FORCES

Divorce. Liberalized divorce laws, including no-fault divorce and incompatibility claims, opened the floodgates. Marriages, previously held together only by tough laws, suddenly dissolved. By the 1970s, the U.S. had the dubious honor of the world's highest divorce rate, with about 40 percent of marriages likely to end in divorce.

Birth control. The introduction of the Pill in the 1960s was perhaps the most important development in America's sexual revolution. Not only did it reduce unplanned pregnancies, it gave women new freedom in their relationships and competition with men, and permitted better planning of their lives—schooling, career, and parenthood.

Education. Several million World War II vets went to college on the G.I. Bill, their ticket to the middle class. They in turn sent their daughters, as well as their sons—the baby boomers—to college. Unlike coeds from previous generations who often went to college to find husbands, this independent group of women, emancipated by the Pill, were bent on pursuing careers. And older women began following their example.

Social Change. The 1960s was an era of 'isms' that altered the way many Americans live, work, play, and think. Amid the ferment of the Vietnam-War protests, student uprisings, the civil-rights movement, and women's liberation, women became convinced that they had more options than being homemakers and forever subordinate to men. A majority of men eventually agreed.

Abortion. There were 587,000 abortions in 1972, the year it was legalized in all 50 states. The number doubled within five years and has been over 1.5 million a year since 1980.

Economy. The economy expanded rapidly during the 1960s and early 1970s, providing jobs and opportunity, and therefore encouragement, for women to pursue careers. Then came two oil embargoes, the hyperinflation of the Carter years, and several recessions. While many women pursued careers and opportunities opened up by affirmative-action efforts, a growing number worked because they had to—to supplement their husbands' income, or because they were the sole breadwinner in the growing number of female-headed households.

What all of this meant for busters was that they had, on average, one brother or one sister, instead of two or three siblings. They had fewer friends in the neighborhood their own age. Their parents, better educated by a few years than previous generations, had waited longer to marry and were a few years older when their first buster baby was born. Those same parents finished their childrearing sooner, too, wrapping it up within 20 or so years, unlike parents of baby boomers who actively parented for 30 or 35 years.

The Baby Recession

After K–8 enrollment topped out nationally in 1969 at 36.7 million, enrollment over the next dozen years plummeted, hitting 31.2 million in the fall of 1983. Inevitably the downward spiral overtook the high schools. From the 1976 high of 15.6 million students (grades 9–12), enrollment fell to 12.5 million by 1990, before starting a slow rise.

THE 1993 U.S. POPULATION

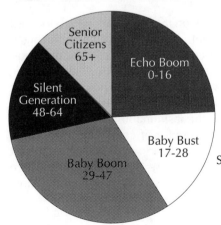

Echo Boom : 63,652,000
Baby Bust : 44,213,000
Baby Boom : 77,640,000
Silent Generation : 39,330,000
Senior Citizens : 32,757,000

17

source: U.S. Bureau of the Census, middle series projections

While school districts tried to tough it out at first, sooner or later they had to start making some painful adjustments and savings. The ranks of K–12 teachers, which had been growing by about 50,000 annually during the baby boom, declined by 44,000 in the late 1970s and early 1980s, totaling 2.4 million in 1981. At the same time, veteran teachers found themselves being bounced from one grade to another, and from one subject to another, as administrators scrambled to reconfigure their schools and faculty.

Nationwide, the layoffs were quite small, and many suburban districts avoided them, finding savings elsewhere. Teacher layoffs hit hardest in northern urban districts, which were grappling with both the baby bust and outmigration.

On the plus side, as enrollment declined, class size and teacher-student ratios also declined. In the spring of 1964, when the first baby boomers were graduating from high school, there were 26 students per teacher. In 1983, when busters began graduating from high school, the K–12 ratio was down to 18 students per teacher. By 1990, the ratio was 17 students per teacher.

When it became clear that the callback he expected was not going to come, Alexander Hardie, like countless other laid-off teachers, reluctantly began looking for another job outside of education. He eventually landed a sales job with a chemical company.

An early story in the *Detroit News* on the baby bust, which focused on the looming layoffs and school closings in districts in Michigan and nationwide, became a point of discussion at a board of education meeting in the upscale Detroit suburb of Birmingham. The school board produced its own projections and reassured parents that, while it might be a national trend, it wasn't expected to affect Birmingham severely, because the fashionable town was a strong magnet for young, professional couples of childbearing age—the massive cohort of baby boomers. The theory was interesting. The fact remains that Birmingham has had to close 7 school buildings since the 1970s, and now operates only 16 schools—all of which illustrates the power of the baby-bust vacuum.

18

While educators grappled with how to respond to declining enrollment, they were also hit with increasingly tight budgets. Federal funding was cut back during the 1980s, shifting a greater burden to the states and communities. Recessions and citizen tax revolts further complicated the perennial funding challenge.

Many districts trimmed costs by closing underutilized school buildings and other facilities and combining schools. That, plus shrinking enrollment, despite the layoffs and appearances of turmoil, actually permitted schools on average to spend more per pupil. The annual expenditure per public school pupil (K–12) in constant 1990–91 dollars was $3,386 in 1970, hovered around $4,300 in the early 1980s, and broke through the $5,000 barrier in 1986, to reach an estimated $5,748 by 1991, according to the National Center for Education Statistics.

The U.S. had 88,600 primary and secondary schools in the mid-1970s. A decade later, 5,000 had been closed, according to the U.S. Department of Education. Parochial schools were also hard hit by declining enrollments. Catholics, whose traditionally large families were downsizing almost as rapidly as the national average, were moving to suburbia and public schools. Among parochial and private schools, mergers became as common and complicated as the mastheads of newspapers whose names became longer, joined by ampersands and different type faces. While the fallout was seen most clearly in the school systems, the ripple effect reached throughout society and hit marketers of youth products especially hard.

Too many marketers—like educators—ignored the initial trends, believing—hoping—that the birth downturn of the mid-1960s was a temporary aberration, perhaps tied to the uneasiness in the wake of the Kennedy assassination, building racial unrest, and the growing involvement in the Vietnam War. After all, births dipped during World War II and then shot up afterwards.

One of the few companies to accurately gauge the impact of the bust and respond quickly was Levi Strauss, whose name is synonymous with blue jeans. The clothing manufacturer met the challenge by expanding its apparel line in the early 1980s to include fuller-cut jeans, maternity clothes, and youthwear, as well as a line of sport coats and suits, all aimed at aging boomers and their own babies. Meanwhile, the company continued to market its traditional snug-fitting jeans, which still appealed to young people who now happened to be baby busters. As a result of a clever marketing strategy that appeals to three groups—boomers, busters and "boomletters"— Levi's sales are higher than ever, reaching $5.6 billion worldwide in 1992—almost two-thirds of that coming from U.S. sales.

19

Unlike boomers, whose power and influence derive from their seeming massive numbers, busters' influence comes from their comparative rarity. In basic economic theory, scarcity drives up the value of a commodity. Therefore, a comparatively small number of busters should have triggered closer attention of marketers selling youth-oriented products.

The basic mistake that marketers and educators, and even some demographers made, was in making straight-line projections, assuming that the past would repeat itself, that women entering the childbearing years in the 1960s and 1970s would have the same number of children as their mothers.

Latchkey Legacy

Not only were busters fewer than boomers, they were decidedly different in many ways, which teachers began noticing when the younger generation began working its way through the school systems.

Carol MacDonald, who taught both boomers and busters in several states, sees a clear difference between the two generations. "Boomers grew up in a secure June Cleaver, Lassie world with the requisite two parents, cat and dog, and station wagon. But then in high school, they were hit by Vietnam, civil rights, Timothy Leary, Watergate. So idealistic my students were, and so active on behalf of a few big, frightening causes."

Boomers were typically self-confident, alternately altruistic and self-indulgent. "Boomers were impatient to get ahead. ... Busters seem reluctant to take the first step," remembers MacDonald, who now teaches in suburban Philadelphia. "Busters have a surfeit of material goods. They've grown up with mountain bikes, microwaves, printers, and so on. These are not either luxuries or necessities. They've just been on the scene for as long as they can remember." Another factor that contributes to the creature comforts of the buster group is the indulgence of grandparents who lavish their grandchildren with big-ticket items.

20

Busters have their causes, to be sure. "They're health conscious. In California, they make it a religion," reports MacDonald, who taught in California before moving to Pennsylvania. "But busters are not big-time activists. While they have a 'Peace Corps' mentality, their concern is very focused in small spheres. And they can do it. They volunteer in inner-city schools, they work in nursing homes and hospitals, they're peer counselors in anti-drug crusades. Or they're involved in animal rights or trying to clean up the streams. They want to continue this volunteerism in college and afterwards."

Busters are busy, not always easy to please, and very independent. "I remember growing up thinking that school was a waste of time. I would say most of my friends thought so, too. That was one reason why a lot of people didn't really work very hard, especially in high school. High school was a bust. And when we went to college, we weren't prepared for it," contends buster Cyndy Wrobel, a 21-year-old college student from Eastpointe, Michigan.

"At home we were kind of taught to think for ourselves and left to our own devices," says Wrobel. "When we had to come to school and they had these rules that you had to follow, it kind of took away the independence you had at home."

Because so many busters' mothers were working, at least part-time, busters were the first generation of latchkey children. Older busters were often home alone in the afternoon, while younger busters waited to be picked up at day-care centers.

The latchkey experience has undoubtedly made these children more independent and self-sufficient at an earlier age than previous generations. For some, depending on their own resources may have even started before the traditional peer pressure associated with elementary school.

While baby boomers were the first generation weaned on TV, busters surpassed even the trendsetting boomers in tube time. It is now estimated that the typical American child logs some 22,000 hours watching television by age 18—more than twice the time spent in school.

What were toddler busters watching? The original Mickey Mouse Club, a quintessential baby-boom show, had been off the air for several years. Instead of a mouse, busters were taking their cues and learning their ABCs from Big Bird on "Sesame Street," which debuted in 1969. Big Bird, Cookie Monster, and Oscar the Grouch have educated and indoctrinated, as well as entertained, an entirely new generation.

More than other shows of its era or before, "Sesame Street" viewed itself as preschool, a fun but effective way to learn and prepare for real school. In addition to teaching the alphabet, simple arithmetic, brotherhood, and good citizenship, "Sesame Street" is also in the vanguard of promoting concern for the environment and the need to protect it, which may help explain why the environment is a hot-button issue with many busters today.

While "Sesame Street" has been largely praised as an educational tool, some critics worry that even such a quality show, and television more generally, has made young viewers passive learners with shortened attention spans, who may lack the discipline needed for rigorous study. But with so many mothers at work, television became a buster babysitter. With the expanded program offerings made available by cable channels, busters can now watch not only the handful of shows that address their own lifestyles—like "Beverly Hills 90210" and "Melrose Place"—but they can also reflect on the childhood of their elders by tuning in to reruns of "The Partridge Family" and "The Brady Bunch."

While their preference might be for sitcoms, younger adult busters can't help but catch the news and unfolding current events, inconveniently wedged between their favorite shows. What they see is dramatically different from what boomers saw in the 1950s and 1960s.

"Just as the experience of Munich cautioned their parents' generation against the appeasement of aggression, so the experience of Vietnam cautioned the baby-boom generation against overcommitment of U.S. power in the world," writes Harvard University professor R. Scott Fosler in *Demographic Change and the American Future.*

"Now another generation of Americans is coming to adulthood with a far more mixed picture of their country's international role. Their adolescent experiences have included an awareness of growing foreign economic competition, repeated attacks on the prestige of the United States abroad in the form of terrorism and the taking of hostages, and the image of Ronald Reagan seeming to stand tall in the world. But it is not apparent that any single event or intense experience has molded their world view."

Some buster-watchers have wondered if the 1986 explosion of the space shuttle *Challenger* wasn't the horrifying frozen moment

22

and loss of innocence for busters that the 1963 assassination of President Kennedy was for boomers.

Interestingly, it was not on the same level. Teacher Carol MacDonald sees a clear difference. "The JFK assassination is permanently etched in our consciousness. That youth and vitality were so vulnerable, that such violence could happen in our country was unthinkable," says MacDonald, vividly recalling where she was on November 22, 1963, when the news broke.

While NASA launches and technology's marvels had become routine for busters, millions of them watched the ill-fated *Challenger* launch on TV at their schools, because a teacher, Christa McAuliffe, was on board for the first time. Within seconds, she and her six fellow astronauts were killed in a bright orange-yellow fireball. Busters were then aged 10 to 21.

"Were the students shocked? Yes. Beyond belief? No. Was the experience a significant one for them? No. They did grieve for the families, but somehow the horror of it didn't seem to go beyond the limits of the TV screen. It still doesn't," contends MacDonald.

"My students then and now are interested in aerospace technology, go to the summer space camp, and still aspire to be astronauts. By and large, they haven't lost confidence in American technology or promise," MacDonald adds.

Her daughter, Lizabeth, a buster, adds: "The *Challenger* explosion was a technological failure. It wasn't a symbol. We moved on."

BUSTER UPPERS AND BUSTER DOWNERS

Year	Upper	Downer
1965	The Bust begins	Power blackout hits Northeast
1966	Dr. Michael De Bakey implants first artificial heart	Racial unrest in Watts, California
1967	First human heart transplant	Riots hit Detroit, other northern cities
1968	President Johnson, who is not seeking re-election, announces he will open peace negotiations with North Vietnam	Martin Luther King, Jr., and Robert Kennedy are assassinated; North Korea seizes *USS Pueblo;* Soviets invade Czechoslovakia
1969	Man on the Moon; underdog N.Y. Mets win the World Series	Ted Kennedy involved in a fatal car crash at Chappaquiddick; U.S. Army Lt. William Calley stands trial for Mylai massacre in Vietnam
1970	Sixties over	Four students slain at Vietnam protest at Kent State University
1971	Voting age lowered to 18; U.S. ping-pong team visits China	Vietnam War spreads to Laos and Cambodia; Attica prison uprising
1972	U.S. resumes diplomatic relations with China	Terrorists hit Munich Olympics
1973	Vietnam cease-fire, U.S. troops withdraw	Watergate hearings; first Arab oil embargo forces lines at gas stations; households cut energy use

Year	Upper	Downer
1974	Watergate nightmare ends with Gerald Ford's appointment as president; Muhammed Ali regains title	Richard Nixon becomes the first U.S. president to resign; Patty Hearst kidnapped
1975	Atari introduces Pong— the first popular arcade computer game; U.S. and Soviet spacecraft link up in space	Two attempts made on life of President Ford; U.S. civilians evacuate Saigon
1976	USA's Bicentennial; Jimmy Carter elected as outsider, reformer	Mysterious Legionnaire's disease kills 29 in Philadelphia
1977	"Roots" becomes most watched TV mini-series; "Star Wars" hits theaters— will become future buster favorite at video stores	New York City hit by 25-hour blackout triggering massive confusion and looting; two jumbo jets collide in Tenerife, Canary Islands, killing 570
1978	Israel's Menachem Begin and Egypt's Anwar El-Sadat sign "Framework for Peace" after 13-day conference organized by President Carter	Italy's Prime Minister Aldo Moro kidnapped and assassinated; Pope Paul VI dies; Pope John Paul I dies after 34 days as pontiff
1979	Margaret Thatcher, England's first woman prime minister, takes office	Iran takes U.S. hostages; Three Mile Island nuclear accident; Soviet invasion of Afghanistan

Year	Upper	Downer
1980	Earth Day attracts over 1 million, including buster environmentalists; feisty Lee Iacocca wins loan, guarantees to keep underdog Chrysler afloat; Ronald Reagan elected president in anti-malaise groundswell	SATs average 890—lowest ever; John Lennon murdered; balanced budget proposals scrapped by congress
1981	MTV launched; longest economic expansion ever (1981–88) begins; Sandra Day O'Connor named first woman justice on the Supreme Court	President Reagan shot; Pope John Paul II shot
1982	*USA Today* launched; Barney Clark gets artificial heart and lives another 3-$\frac{1}{2}$ months	AIDS discovered
1983	*The Right Stuff* movie debuts—a hit with many busters who aspire to become astronauts	237 U.S. Marines killed in Beirut; KAL airliner shot down by Soviets
1984	Busters vote in presidential election for first time; Geraldine Ferraro named Democrats' VP candidate	Federal cuts to school aid
1985	Shortage of new workers develops, bidding up wages of busters	Walker/Pollard spy cases

Year	Upper	Downer
1986	"Ferris Bueller's Day Off" premieres—busters flock to see it	NASA space shuttle _Challenger_ explodes, killing all seven astronauts
1987	National Association for the Advancement of Time, an anti-boomer group, launched—raises buster issues, gripes	Insider trading scandal; stock market plunges
1988	Busters big in pro sports	Pan Am flight 103 blows up over Lockerbie, Scotland
1989	Berlin Wall falls	_Exxon Valdez_ oil spill; Tiananmen Square crackdown on Chinese dissidents
1990	Soviet satellite nations gain independence, pursue democratic reforms; Nelson Mandela freed; 41 nations ban ocean dumping	Recession begins; tension builds between U.S. and Iraq— war likely
1991	Desert Storm victory; Russia gets its first freely elected leader—Boris Yeltsin; _Generation X_ published; TV's "thirtysomething" cancelled; recession officially ends	Rodney King beating; Clarence Thomas hearings; NBA star Magic Johnson reveals he has AIDS
1992	Buster and boomer launch "Lead ... Or Leave" campaign; presidential candidate Bill Clinton listens	L.A. riots erupt after verdict in Rodney King beating case; U.S. unemployment hits 7.4%
1993	President Clinton takes first step to fix Social Security— proposes raising taxes on benefits to upper-income recipients	President Clinton doesn't go far enough in Social Security changes—still needs major overhaul

27

source: _American Demographics_ magazine;
The 1993 Information Please Almanac Facts on File

Not only have busters grown up logging extraordinary amounts of tube time, they are also grabbing the nearest joystick to battle outer-space invaders and bad-guy earthlings in the latest computer game. "They seem to spend more time alone. And I think the computer might be linked to that to some extent. Computers and video games, remember they're the video-game generation also, are solitary activities," suggests computer expert Erick Wujcik, who has written extensively about the computer revolution. "They are, more than any other generation in American history, I think, game players. They play electronic games, arcade games, computer games, what have you. This is the generation of kids raised on games."

This baby-bust generation also got into fantasy role-playing games, which first appeared in the late 1970s, with games like *Dungeons and Dragons* and the sci-fi thriller *Traveler.* For some, the games were not only challenges, but escapes from the reality of their home life. There is a better than 50-50 chance that the buster child has spent at least one year in a single-parent household situation before reaching age 18, due to divorce, separation, or widowhood, according to Census Bureau estimates.

"Since 1972, more than 1 million children each year have seen their parents divorce, a threefold increase since 1950. But the percentage of children whose parents divorce has risen even faster. In the 1950s, only 6 out of every 1,000 children experienced parental divorce in a given year, but in the 1980s, this rate varied between 17 and 19 per 1,000," reports Census Bureau demographer Suzanne M. Bianchi in *America's Children: Mixed Prospects* (Population Reference Bureau, 1990).

"In 1960, 88 percent of children lived with two parents, but by 1988, this percentage had dropped to 73. But only about 60 percent lived with their two biological parents in 1988; the remainder lived with a parent and step-parent."

A youngster's home situation has a direct impact on his or her school performance. A higher proportion of busters repeated grades than did previous generations. The newsletter *TechnoPolitics Report* noted in its October 1992 issue that one in four children living in a female-headed household repeat a grade, compared with only one in nine youngsters living with both parents.

"The longer the time spent in a single-parent family, the greater the reduction in education attainment. The effect was more pronounced for boys than for girls," report Sheila Fitzgerald Krein and Andrea H. Beller in the May 1988 issue of *Demography.*

• VOX BUSTER •

"Many of us in this 'lost generation' are the byproducts of boomers. For the past 18 to 24 years, boomers have not been overly concerned about their children's welfare. My generation might not be so apathetic and ill-informed had our parents guided us in being 'better Americans.' ... [The babyboom generation] has refused to accept its civic responsibilities, refused or neglected to rear its children to be doers, and has left a big mess for the 'lost generation' and those after it to clean up. ... "

excerpt of a letter to the editor of Insight magazine
from Cyndy Wrobel, 21, Eastpointe, Michigan

While family size has remained small since the late 1960s, the baby bust ended in 1976, followed by what's been called the echo boom or baby boomlet. For once, demographers saw this trend coming and predicted an upswing in births in the late 1970s and 1980s. Births kept rising steadily through 1990, when they totaled 4,158,212, a 28-year high. In 1991 and 1992, births dropped a bit, but remained above 4 million. While expecting the rise in births, demographers were surprised by its length and how high it went.

Many echo boomers are children of the original baby boomers, who are averaging about two children per couple. What's triggered the increase in births is the fact that there have been so many boomers in the childbearing years. After years of postponing marriage and motherhood to finish school and launch their careers, boomer women began racing their biological clocks, triggering a recent jump in births. Inevitably, births will decline in the 1990s as the baby-boom women pass out of the childbearing years.

Smart school systems, which rented out excess space during the baby-bust years, converted school buildings back to classrooms from their temporary duty as senior and recreational centers and city hall annexes. Shortsighted districts that had sold off buildings were forced to buy portables or hastily put up new buildings to accommodate the echo boom.

One result of the boomlet: Alexander Hardie was recalled in 1985 at age 48 by the South Redford school district after a five-year layoff. "It was just a game of numbers ... Other teachers were retiring and student enrollment began increasing. That's the reason I got called back," Hardie explains.

"I'm noticing that the kids that I had in school in my first years of teaching are now finished with college and getting married. They're moving back into the district. I'm teaching their kids now."

CHAPTER FOUR

Conspicuous Consumers

Busters shop early and often, usually at the mall. They're ravenous consumers, but smart and demanding buyers. They've had plenty of experience.

The comparative size of the baby bust is at the very heart of the advantages and disadvantages of being a buster.

Point: With fewer brothers and sisters, busters had less competition for their parents' attention and resources than did boomers.

Counter point: Since half of busters' mothers held down jobs, they probably saw less of their mothers than did boomers.

Counter-counter point: With the added money they brought into the household and the guilt they felt about leaving the kiddies, mothers (and fathers) lavished more toys, clothes, and other possessions on their buster offspring.

"When children are born to older parents (perhaps 30 plus), they are treasured more," confirms James McNeal in his book *Kids As Customers*. "The growth in financial ability during postponement allows the parents to demonstrate this worth by providing the kids with more. When the kids reach the wanting age, these parents tend to be more responsive."

31

Children are instinctive psychologists when it comes to playing on the guilt of their parents. Materially, at least, busters had it easier growing up than baby boomers did. The exceptions are children raised in female-headed households, where the incidence of poverty is much greater than in two-parent homes.

It cost moderate-income parents of a baby boomer born in 1957 $23,955 to raise that child to age 18, according to the U.S. Department of Agriculture. Babies born in the last year of the baby bust, 1976, cost their parents more than twice that, not including college.

In 1991, the USDA estimated it would cost moderate-income parents $124,890 in current dollars to raise a child born that year to age 18. If those parents then had the misfortune of sending their bright child to an Ivy League college without a scholarship, it could cost them at least another $80,000. No wonder parents have begun rediscovering the joy of state universities.

Yesterday's Luxuries, Today's Essentials

Inflation is only a part of the explanation for the rising cost of kids. Another factor is that many things that are now considered essential or routine in a child's upbringing were luxuries or didn't exist a few decades ago: disposable diapers, car seats, protective headgear, day-care, nannies, interactive educational toys, calculators, computer gear, compact disks, microwaves, cellular phones, and on and on.

Kids have also developed increasingly expensive tastes. Instead of high-top black Keds or P.F. Flyer sneakers that parents bought boomers in the 1950s, buster kids are more likely to be racing around in expensive Reeboks, Nikes, or Topsiders.

As a Joplin, Missouri, mechanic and father of a buster said in a 1990 story in *USA Today:* "Most of my jeans I buy at Wal-Mart. To me, they're the same jeans—just 20 to 30 bucks less. My boy's just the opposite. He likes the high-dollar stuff. He'll go out and pay $70 for a pair of tennis shoes, which to me is stupid. When I get tennis shoes, I pay $15—suits me just fine."

Busters are not ones for self-denial or no-name knock-offs. Labels on the clothes that boomers wore during their childhoods often read Macy's, Sears, or MacGregor, and were hidden on the inside. By the 1970s and 1980s, busters, or more precisely their mothers, were buying clothes with the labels and logos advertised on the outside: snapping alligators, a lamb with its hooves dangling, mallet-swinging guys atop polo ponies. The preppy look that was popular with successful young adults in the 1980s was downsized for their yuppie puppies.

One big reason why many young busters dress so well is that their parents are finally dressing better. Here's why: during their own childhoods, many future parents of busters were outfitted in generic, boring, but sturdy outfits by thrifty parents who grew up during the Depression and knew how to stretch a budget. Perhaps in reaction to that, as the future parents of busters grew independent of their own parents, many adult boomers began trading up in what they bought for themselves and their families. As one advertising campaign for L'Oréal hair products, featuring boomer Cybil Shepherd, put it: "You're worth it."

Naturally, as young adults started spending more on themselves, they inevitably began spending more on their children. Cheryl Russell, a demographer and author of *100 Predictions for the Baby Boom,* notes: "Married couples with kids are spending as much on clothes as couples without kids. But those with kids are spending it on children's clothes."

Not surprisingly, buster kids became brand-conscious—if not brand loyal—from an early age, able to distinguish one designer's clothes from another at a distance of 30 yards, the way car-crazy youths have always been able to identify cars by their headlights two blocks away.

Born to Shop; Primed to Spend

I, a baby boomer, got my first bike—actually a red tricycle—handed down from my older brother, to be turned over to my younger boomer sister. I graduated at age six to my first two-wheeler, a functional 20-inch Huffy Convertible, with one gear and balloon tires. My next bike was a 26-inch Denault English racer with three gears, which I was still riding when I was old enough to have a driver's license.

Instead of indestructible, high-riding trikes that lasted through 3.7 siblings, busters first tooled around the neighborhood and down their driveways on low-riding plastic Big Wheels and Hot Wheels, which were great for going into controlled slides. But the hollow wheels wore through in time, seldom lasting beyond one child's Big Wheel phase.

33

If not their first authentic two-wheeler, then certainly busters' second bike was likely a lightweight alloy road racer, with 10 gears, two hand brakes, dropped handlebars for better aerodynamics, and adjustable stirrup toe-holds. The crash helmet, racing shorts and shirt, and metal clip shoes came separately. The total on the cash register for all this can easily top $600. Some bikes cost $1,000 to 2,000 alone.

As for their photographic gear, busters quickly graduated from Instamatic cameras to 35-mm imports, which offered color photographs, albeit often out-of-focus ones in the hands of such young paparazzi. Their parents had video gear and cassette recorders to record their every move and sound.

SPENDING BY 12-to-19-YEAR-OLDS

Spending in billions on:

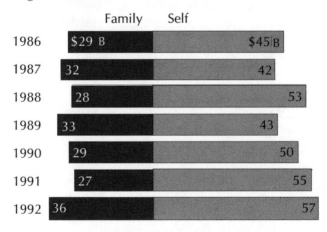

	Family	Self
1986	$29 B	$45 B
1987	32	42
1988	28	53
1989	33	43
1990	29	50
1991	27	55
1992	36	57

source: TRU's Teenage Marketing & Lifestyle Study
© 1992, Teenage Research Unlimited, Northbrook, Illinois

Pretty soon, busters were buying for themselves, and not just overpriced toys advertised on Saturday morning TV. When boomers Joe and Michele Rossmann, of Centreville, Virginia, drove their 18-year-old buster son, Brian, off to James Madison University in the fall of 1992, they had to take two cars.

"It was either that or having to rent a U-Haul," says Mrs. Rossmann. "It did take two. We're talking computer and stereo with CD player, clothes, sports equipment, soccer ball, tennis racket, probably ten pairs of shoes, including athletic shoes. ... The roommate brought the refrigerator and a television."

Brian's wardrobe included nine or ten pairs of jeans and twice as many T-shirts. His father, vice-president of employee benefits for a trade association, and his mother, a registered nurse, returned two weeks later with his 10-speed bike and some baked goodies.

In contrast, Mrs. Rossmann recalls that when she left for her first year at the Southern Illinois University in the fall of 1968, she took only two suitcases and a typewriter. "I must not have had very many things."

To their dismay, Brian and his roommate discovered that they lacked a telephone-answering machine. Brian also had to leave behind his black 1984 Mazda RX7, which sister Megan, an 18-year-old high school senior, gladly inherited.

"They [busters] are ravenous consumers," observes Bruce Elliott, who has informally studied, surveyed, and written about busters. "It is the busters who wear the $200 sneakers. They have ravenous appetites out of proportion to their numbers. Yes, they will be worth marketing to. At the same time, they're nobody's fool."

Consider these impressive results of a national Roper CollegeTrack survey, which is representative of the busters in college full-time in 1991:

- 86 percent have a car; 41 percent plan to buy a new car within the next two years.
- 60 percent have a credit card; 70 percent have an automatic teller machine card; and 55 percent have a telephone credit card.
- 63 percent have their own TV; one in three has their own microwave and VCR; one in four has a computer.
- Half have traveled by airplane in the last year.

Several of these items or services, which are now commonplace to busters, barely existed—if at all—during boomers' college years.

35

Additionally, a higher proportion of busters work during their school years than did boomers, providing busters with more spending money and bigger bank accounts. Roper CollegeTrack calculates that the typical buster undergraduate in 1992 had personal buying power of $4,840 annually, with discretionary spending of $138 per month.

Teenage Research Unlimited of Northbrook, Illinois, calculates that youngsters aged 12 to 19 spent an estimated $93 billion in 1992. Of that, $36 billion was money given to them to spend on family needs, such as shopping for groceries and other errands. The remaining $57 billion was money that teens spent on themselves. In 1986, by contrast, TRU estimated that teen spending totaled $74 billion, of which $29 billion was spent on the household and $45 billion was spent on themselves.

Various ways of calculating young Americans' discretionary spending yield different totals. The one thing they all have in common is the clear fact that busters represent a multi-billion dollar audience. "They're taking over more and more of the family shopping," says Peter Zollo, president of Teenage Research Unlimited. "That's due to the increase in dual-income and single-parent families. Whether they like it or not, teens are the only family members with time to spend in a shopping line."

Professor James McNeal, in his book *Kids as Customers,* says that children in single-parent homes "are expected to assume more of the role of partner and to perform some of the consumer-related tasks that the missing parent might ordinarily do—shopping, preparing meals, feeding pets, cleaning house. The net result is that kids handle more money, often at an earlier age, buy more for themselves, and buy more for the household."

In dual-income households, McNeal finds that "parents also tend to ask their kids to do more around the house and to be more self-reliant. This, in turn, requires the youngsters to assume the consumer role more frequently and probably at an earlier age."

Trend trackers Lawrence Graham and Lawrence Hamdan's estimate of young adults' discretionary income is proclaimed in the title of their 1987 book, *YouthTrends: Capturing the $200 Billion Youth Market.* Defining youth as people aged 13 to 25, they write, "Young adults have incomes totaling nearly $200 billion annually, according to data from the Census Bureau, studies by *Business Week, Newsweek,* and *Advertising Age,* and figures from Simmons Market Research Bureau and the Rand Youth Poll. Teenagers have $50 to $55 billion to spend; college students, $35 to $45 billion; and noncollege young adults,

$100 to $115 billion." Between 1987 and 1993, inflation may have boosted the total by another $25 to $50 billion.

If one looks at busters who are heading their own households, the Bureau of Labor Statistics estimates that in 1990 there were 7.6 million households in which the household head was under age 25. Those households had an average annual expenditure of $16,518 and a combined total expenditure of $125 billion.

No matter how one calculates the spending of busters, their spending will only rise as they get older, take on more responsibility and expenses, become more established in their careers, and increase their incomes.

• VOX BUSTER •

"We're very independent, because our moms started off raising us, and then suddenly there was this movement for women to get their independence or go to work. Or financially, the mom had to go back to work. So, we had to make it on our own, learn to do our homework by ourselves. And when we had to start getting jobs, we had to start paying for things, so we could have clothes. So, in that sense we're independent. I think we maybe live beyond our means, because I have several friends who within a year's time got themselves into big-time credit-card trouble. We're maybe not fiscally responsible. I think we want at least what our parents had."

—Cyndy Wrobel, 21, Eastpointe, Michigan

Mall Babies

While busters may have expensive tastes, they know how and where to shop to get what they want. They've had plenty of experience. Busters are the first generation exposed from their earliest years to malls—a consumer cornucopia.

"The mall is a common experience for the majority of American youth; they have probably been going there all their lives," writes William Severini Kowinski in his 1985 book, *The Malling of America.* "Some ran within their first large open space, saw their first fountain, bought their first toy, and read their first book in a mall. They may have smoked their first cigarette or first joint or turned them down, had their first kiss or lost their virginity in the mall parking lot. Teenagers in America now spend more time in the mall than anywhere else but home and school. Mostly, it is their choice, but some of that mall time is put in as the result of two-paycheck and single-parent households and the lack of other viable alternatives."

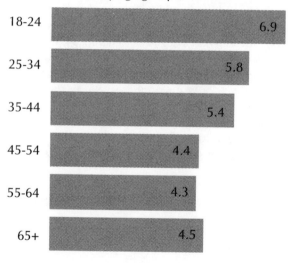

"LET'S GO SHOPPING"

Average number of shopping center visits per month, by age group

Age group	Visits
18-24	6.9
25-34	5.8
35-44	5.4
45-54	4.4
55-64	4.3
65+	4.5

source: International Council of Shopping Centers
and the Gallup Organization, 1990

Malls—initially surprised by the invasion of teenagers—did a survey of their young patrons. The study, conducted by the Gallup Organization and published by the International Council of Shopping Centers (ICSC), reveals that "the vast majority support the same set of values as does shopping-center management."

Writes Kowinski: "The 'same set of values' means simply that mall kids are already preprogrammed to be consumers and that the mall can put the finishing touches to them as hard-core, lifelong shoppers just like everybody else. That, after all, is what the mall is about. So it shouldn't be surprising that in spending a lot of time there, adolescents find little that challenges the assumption that the goal of life is to make money and buy products, or that just about everything else in life is to be used to serve those ends."

Cyndy Wrobel, a 21-year-old college student who grew up in the Detroit suburb of Eastpointe, recalls mall excursions with her friends. "Our parents used to drop us off at the mall when we couldn't drive. And then when we could drive, we just went on our own. It was like a Saturday afternoon outing-type deal. We'd go shopping we might go to the movies and we'd go to lunch. We'd be there maybe a good six hours. You know kids today do that, and even more, I've noticed."

The 1990 ICSC survey found that 18-to-24-year-olds were the shoppingest age group of adults there is. They made an average of seven visits per month to a shopping center, at least one more visit than baby boomers made. The average number of visits for all age groups was five trips per month.

While the ICSC includes strip centers as well as malls in its shopping-center definition, 18-to-24-year-olds are the most likely to shop at a mall—83 percent of their shopping trips are to full-fledged malls, as opposed to strip centers. Only 19 percent prefer traditional down-town shops.

There are about 31,500 shopping centers across the United States, of which 2,500 are enclosed malls. According to the Gallup survey, over half of busters described their shopping trips as recreation. But busters also like to shop. Unlike boomers who now must shop for their children as well as themselves, busters, most of whom are still unmarried, are often buying for themselves.

Shop 'til They Drop; Working to Pay for It   39

Unencumbered by financial responsibilities, busters are doing their concerted best to stimulate the economy—shopping 'til they drop. Many work to earn money to shop. "I shop, therefore I am." They are in the acquisitive stage of life.

"Twentysomething women love to shop. And shop they do. The vast majority of these women consider shopping something to do; they seem to think of it almost as a favorite hobby," according to *Twentysomething: The New Individual.* The 1992 report, which was prepared by The Roper Organization for *Mademoiselle* magazine, continues: "Independent and indulgent, twentysomething women love to splurge on themselves, presumably for their hard work. Rather than saving to attain the impossible dream, they spend big on life's little luxuries—such as clothes, accessories, cosmetics, toiletries, entertainment, and getaways."

Who sells all these goods to busters? It's other busters, working as clerks in part-time positions sandwiched between classes. Busters are buying from busters who speak the same language, know each others' tastes, and trust one another.

Megan Rossmann, an 18-year-old high school senior from Centreville, Virginia, has had after-school jobs since she was 15. "Basically, I do it for extra money. A lot of my friends work, too. It's just, you know, like pocket-money-type things."

For a few months during her junior year, Megan was holding down two part-time jobs at the same time. "I used to save. But a lot of times, I've been going on trips with my friends. Usually, I don't ask my parents for money then. I use my own," says Megan. She laughingly adds that on more than one occasion her parents have come to her for a quick loan.

In addition to the malls, fast-food restaurants are a prime source of jobs (and food) for busters. McDonald's, the industry leader, is justly proud of the fact that its 8,000-plus restaurants employ 1 in 15 first-time job holders. While annual turnover is 100 percent, the golden arches employ some 500,000 people—mostly teens—at any one time. McDonald's alumni number about 8 million, according to a 1989 article in *Policy Review* by Ben Wildavsky titled "McJobs." Assuming most of those people are still in the work force, that means that 6 percent of the entire U.S. labor force has worked at McDonald's at some time in their lives.

40

For a variety of reasons, the proportion of busters who work at McDonald's and throughout the fast-food industry, as well as at the malls and elsewhere during their high school and college years, is higher than it was for boomers—not just during summer vacation, but throughout the year.

A 1990 national survey by Harris/Scholastic Research of 10,051 high school juniors and seniors found that fully half had part-time jobs during the school year; 3 percent worked full-time. "Employment appears to be an integral part of the lives of high school juniors and seniors, with more than half of them currently working and two in five looking for work," notes the summary of the survey, which was conducted for the U.S. Army Recruiting Command. "Academic standing has no effect on the likelihood of young people to be employed after school."

Because of cutbacks in federal grants and increases in student loans during the 1980s, many busters worked during high school, and later, during college, to pay their college tuition. Many, no doubt, also worked to get enough money to buy the things they wanted: cars, stereos, computers, clothes, bikes, cameras, and such.

This early exposure to work and the business world during the go-go years of the early and mid-1980s may explain the rapid increase in college freshmen expressing an interest in pursuing business careers after graduation. The proportion rose from 12 percent in 1966 to a peak of 25 percent by 1987, according to *The American Freshman: National Norms for Fall 1991*. The survey is conducted by the Higher Education Research Institute, University of California.

Since then, and in the wake of the S&L scandals and Wall Street and corporate turmoil of the late 1980s, interest in business careers has dropped to 16 percent of freshmen in 1991, according to *The American Freshman* report, still several points above the baby-boom averages of the 1960s.

The actual choice of a business major has followed a similar trendline. Interest in majoring in business fell from a peak of 27 percent of freshmen in 1987 to 18 percent in 1991. Despite the decline, business remains the most popular degree.

Finding after-school and summer jobs has been easier for busters than boomers. Boomers, by their sheer numbers, presented stiff competition to one another for their first part-time jobs. Two of my own boyhood friends may have invented the concept of job sharing, as they split one job in half. Each worked 20 hours a week, tending a municipal tennis court one summer. Busters were looking for after-school and summer jobs for the most part during a period when jobs were both growing rapidly and moving to where they were—in the suburbs. The economy was shifting toward services, which required part-time workers. Plus, kids had grown increasingly independent of their preoccupied parents, even more so than boomers. A job was no longer viewed as some onerous pubescent obligation or rite of passage, but as a bit of drudgery to be endured to earn money and the freedom and possessions it brings.

Where many boomers, during the Vietnam era, were challenging capitalism as well as the war, busters a decade later were budding entrepreneurs, committed capitalists, and consumers in training.

The bottom line: "When all of these social forces occur together, as they did during the 1980s, the result is a better-heeled, more self-reliant, more market-mature child," says marketing professor James McNeal in *Kids as Customers*. "She or he is not only better off financially than the 1970s kid, but knows a lot more about being a consumer and knows it at an earlier age."

PART II

This Is Now

• •

CHAPTER FIVE

Computer Jocks and Cyberheads

Baby busters are the first generation to grow up with computers, using them at home, school, and on the job. Unintimidated by technology, they don't see what all the fuss is about.

When buster Tom Herman encountered his first computer as a high school sophomore over a dozen years ago, he wasn't sure what it did. The IBM-XT was bigger than his parents' color TV set. "I think what I was thinking of was games. That's pretty much what I thought computers did back then—just play games," admits Herman. He soon learned better during his first computer course that year; he mastered computers during college and graduate studies.

These days, Herman nonchalantly sits in front of three computers at his office in suburban Syracuse, New York, doing analysis on distribution networks and existing and proposed store locations. "I wouldn't be doing what I'm doing now if I didn't know computers inside and out, that's for sure," says Herman, senior market research analyst for Fay's Incorporated, a drugstore chain. "There's not a single department in this company that's not dependent on computers."

Diana Detwiler, a 25-year-old buster from southern California, recalls using a computer almost exclusively to write term papers at Princeton University, until she went looking for a job. "Employers asked, 'Do you know Lotus; do you know spreadsheet programs?' And I hadn't even heard of them."

After getting some quick instruction at her university's computer center, Detwiler went on to teach herself even more before landing a job with a Los Angeles bank. "I was in leveraged financing. We did financial modeling on the computer, using Lotus. We needed computers," says Detwiler. In the two years she was at the bank, her department went through three generations of computers.

While older busters like Detwiler and Herman first encountered computers in high school or college, many younger busters have practically grown up with computers. Says Herman: "Now people are starting even in elementary school."

"I saw it as something new, something you learn from. We did everything from play games to write reports on them," recalls Jason Palmer, an Oklahoman who met up with his first computer in fourth grade. By seventh grade, he and a classmate created an educational computer game based on the Bill of Rights, which earned them third place in a statewide computer competition.

Now 21, Palmer divides his time between working at a gas station and studying at Southwestern Oklahoma University, using a computer at both places. While his baby-boomer boss at the gas station admits to being afraid of the new computer, Palmer mastered it quickly by reading the 200-page manual one night and now uses it routinely and casually.

In college, in addition to using computers for class assignments, Palmer has been accessing vast database networks to analyze graduation rates and job-placement records of various graduate schools, starting salaries of graduates, and starting salaries offered by various companies in a methodical effort to determine where to do graduate work in engineering two years from now. He'll also choose his engineering subspecialty based on where the computer tells him the opportunities are.

"In my day and time, I'd say the computer is a 'have to,'" contends Palmer. "It's made a big impact on my life. It makes it easier for a person to access information. Instead of going from book to book, you can access it and basically get all of your information at once. You get a printout and you're ready to go."

45

Computerease

Contrast Palmer's experience and attitude with that of baby boomers, like his 47-year-old boss Ron Goodman, who first encountered computers and had to adapt to them as adults. Goodman's Phillips 66 gas station in Weatherford, Oklahoma, was just equipped with computers for billing and inventory control. "He's not afraid to punch the buttons. And, boy, I am," says Goodman, comparing himself with his younger employee.

In a society and workplace that is increasingly computerized, author and computer expert Erick Wujcik says of busters: "Kids in this generation have the advantage of not having any fear of computers and that's a biggie. That's huge. They don't have the computer phobia that their predecessors have had."

For many busters, early exposure to computers came at home, where parents, who may not have known how to operate computers themselves, nevertheless bought them for their young children. The kids started out on computers playing video games, subconsciously learning how to operate computers while having fun. Basically, a lot of what busters know about computers has been self-taught.

Mike Vazquez was 8 years old and a sci-fi fan when he spotted a computer in a shop window back in 1978. "I didn't even know what it was. There was sort of a Star Trek space thing just on the screen of the computer," he recalls. "I told my dad I wanted a computer, initially just for the games aspect."

Mike got a *Detroit News* paper route with 250 customers to earn enough money to get the computer. After a year, he had $500 in the bank. His father matched it, allowing him to buy a $1,000 Atari.

"Then I started taking some classes at Oakland Community College in fourth or fifth grade. And I taught myself Basic.... Certainly more than any of my contemporaries at the time, I knew how to make a computer work and had experience through a broad range of applications," recalls Vazquez, now 24 and a Harvard graduate.

"I was just intoxicated by the idea of having a computer with games at home. I was typical of a certain segment of my generation in that

I was really into Star Wars, really into sci-fi stuff when I was real young. The first book I read was *The Hobbit* by J.R.R. Tolkien. And I also hung out in the arcade a lot."

From his earliest days, he also turned to his computer to write and keep a journal. "I always feel very comfortable writing on a computer. It's sort of personal space for me. And that was definitely something that was true then." Since graduating from Harvard, Vazquez has edited two *Let's Go* travel books, which are written by Harvard students. He's currently an editor in the university's Afro-American Studies Department. "I do use computers a lot. I'm using a modem to interface databases and word-processing stuff on an IBM."

While concerned parents with a few thousand dollars to spare were buying their children and themselves computers, companies like IBM and Apple were giving computers away free to schools in hopes of developing future customers.

"With the shrinking cost of computer power, sales of personal computers for educational use took off in 1980–81 and didn't stop. Governments and companies rushed to put personal computers in every school, and parents panicked if their child's school hadn't gotten one. Computer manufacturers queued up to sell or give away their products," writes Tom Forester in *High-Tech Society*.

"There was much talk of 'computer literacy' and the 'keyboard generation.' It was said that computer literacy would take its place alongside the 3 Rs of reading, writing and 'rithmetic as the fourth key skill, and that computers in schools might soon replace pencils," continues Forester, an Australian professor of computer science. "*Time* magazine in 1982 ran a cover story on the remarkable phenomenon of 'The Microkids'—the new computer-literate generation who were more at home in front of a VDT screen than a children's book and who knew more about computers than their parents—and even their teachers. Some also discovered the 'computer toddlers' and the 'preschool software' market, while 'computer camps' (replacing summer camps) enjoyed a mini-boom."

By 1989, 97 percent of K–12 schools were equipped with microcomputers for classroom instruction. That's up from 18 percent in 1981, according to Market Data Retrieval in Shelton, Connecticut.

47

Unlike their elders, many busters have practically been weaned on computers. This could prove a significant strength in the marketplace for busters whose early exposure to computers has given them a head start in coping with new technology.

But while computers are a tremendous educational tool, they are not without liabilities. "One of the things that the television and some of the technology has done to our students is make them very passive learners," says Loretta Schmidt, curriculum director at Weatherford Public Schools in central Oklahoma. "It [computers] makes it very one-on-one, and it doesn't create any interaction between the students, any verbal skills."

• VOX BUSTER •

"We're not afraid of it. Right? That seems to be the main problem of technology. But, if you're exposed to something when you're young, it doesn't scare you. ... For an awful lot of people my age, because we were using computers when we were young, they weren't that intimidating. I'm sure it's a strength. Most people who I know who are working are doing stuff that involves computers. ... There are some [older] people who are so freaked out by using a computer that they can only learn to do one or two things. You can give them a couple of basic directions, and they can use it. But they really don't feel comfortable playing around with it and trying to figure out how it works. I don't have any sort of fetishistic problem with computers. It's just something I use."

—Michael Vazquez, 24, Boston, Massachusetts

And while computers let students access vast amounts of information, some busters may be drowning in a flood of data. "With information doubling like it is now, the baby busters will be the ones who learn to access information. They may not be able to internalize it all," Schmidt contends. "We've come to the conclusion there's no way we can cover it all. So therefore we have to start giving them skills for acquisition, so that they can begin to choose what skills they are going to need. And, if so, how to train themselves to access information and process information to gain the needed skills."

Many students who have used computers extensively in their course work wouldn't survive the first round of a fifth-grade spelling bee, because many software programs have built-in spellcheckers. Similarly, many busters have difficulty with basic math, such as division and percentages, because it is easier to push a button on the computer keyboard and have the computer do the work.

Wujcik, Detwiler, and others warn that while computers may open opportunities for those who do develop computer skills, the technology could also be a barrier for busters and other generations who are not computer literate.

"The whole job market is turning to a situation where in the next 10 or 20 years, it's just going to be assumed that you understand and know how to deal with this technology. And if you don't, you are going to be excluded from that marketplace, unless you already have a track record," contends Wujcik. "The kids who have a facility with these things are going to have an inside track. But the kids who don't are going to have tremendous problems."

Busters' exposure to computers has not been uniform throughout the generation. In many cases, the financial budget of a school system and individual families determined when and how much a child was exposed to computers.

Macworld, in a damning investigation in its September 1992 issue, argues that the statistics showing dramatic gains in computers and their use in schools are misleading and that the many success stories routinely cited ignore clear areas of neglect. "'Even if there were one computer per classroom,' says Herb Lin of the National Academy of Sciences, 'that's less than two minutes per student for a one-hour class.' Insufficient for any meaningful training," according to *Macworld,* a leading magazine covering computer technology.

In a five-month nationwide investigation of computer usage in schools, "America's Shame: The Creation of a Technological Underclass in America's Public Schools," *Macworld* found many schools with antiquated computers, broken and unused equipment, and computers that were used more for games or rote drills than

49

creative and challenging instruction. Furthermore, many teachers were unprepared to use the computers in their classrooms. There was also much evidence of mismanaged or misdirected policies and lesson plans.

National averages tend to understate progress where it has occurred and obscure that fact where it hasn't. *Macworld*, perhaps not surprisingly, found that students from middle- and upper-income towns with better-funded school districts tended to have much more experience and facility with computers than students from impoverished areas. Just as important as what's happening at school, or perhaps more so, is what's happening at home. The higher the income and educational level of parents, the more likely it is that their children will be exposed to computers at home.

Says Detwiler: "There are going to be a large number of people below the minimum, because they just aren't getting those computer skills in school. That's largely due to the lack of computer hardware, because schools just can't afford to buy it. Especially with the current budget cuts, they're not going to be able to buy it any time soon."

Prompted by her concern, Detwiler left banking and in 1991 launched the Computers for Schools program in the San Jose, California, area, through which she encourages companies to donate excess and outmoded computer gear to local schools. "There are a lot of businesses out there that have one-generation-old computer equipment that they have upgraded from and they just don't know what to do with it. It ends up sitting in storerooms and not being used until it's fully depreciated and so old that it's useless." Detwiler has gone to those companies and salvaged the equipment. In her first year, she collected 800 pieces of computer gear, which is now being used by students in San Jose.

Meanwhile, IBM and Apple keep giving computers to schools across the country. In addition to donations of equipment directly to schools by both companies, Apple has spent some $12 million to set up 100 Apple Classrooms of Tomorrow at public schools as laboratories for cutting-edge immersion in computer education.

50

Among other programs designed to make computers available to students are those instituted by supermarket rivals Safeway and Giant. Both have programs encouraging shoppers to donate cash-register receipts to their favorite schools, which the schools can then redeem for discounted computers.

Despite the remaining gaps and challenges, use of computers is rising, typically in inverse proportion to age. A Census Bureau study found that by 1989, 36 percent of those aged 18 to 34 used computers, compared with 28 percent of all persons older than age 18. The proportion was 47 percent for those aged 15 to 17 and over 60 percent for those aged 9 to 13.

"You have a lot of very young people with access to immense amounts of information through their computer. You can have an encyclopedia at your fingertips. You can communicate with your peers for scientific experiments, school reports, or whatever," maintains Diana Detwiler. "Students can identify their areas of interest and areas where they excel, and focus in on those."

For his part, Erick Wujcik believes that early exposure to computers develops a person's analytical skills. "If you've been raised playing video games, arcade games, computer games, and role-playing games, you are a problem solver, much more than someone of the baby-boom generation. People in our boomer generation tend to be people who accepted what was given to them and then en masse revolted against it."

A growing number of jobs and opportunities in the 1990s and into the 21st century will involve computers. "There is an oversupply of jobs for people who are computer literate and have a great facility with computers," contends Detwiler. But Detwiler hastens to add: "There are too many people that don't have those skills. And they're competing for a shrinking fraction of the jobs that don't require computer skills."

Computer literacy will be to the 21st century what the ability to read and write was to the 20th century: an absolute basic prerequisite in society. When compared with their elders, busters have the computer advantage, if only they seize it and build on it.

Tough Times—Tough Marks

When busters were in elementary and high schools, teachers were being laid off in some districts, and underutilized classroom buildings were being closed and schools consolidated. This was initially due to declining enrollments and later to tight budgets. School districts scrambled for funds. The proportion of money coming from the federal government has declined since the late 1970s, putting a heavier burden on states and local communities.

Especially strapped were those northern towns and cities losing families to the Sunbelt, which accelerated the enrollment decline up north. Fewer families meant declining property tax revenues, a major source of school funding. Fewer students meant a decline in those funds based on enrollment.

Puzzled administrators, who only a decade before were recruiting furiously and opening new buildings every few years, were now shuffling staff and resources and selling off buildings.

SCHOOLS WITH COMPUTERS; STUDENTS WITH ACCESS

Public Schools

Year	% with Microcomputers	Students/Computer
1983	68.4%	92.3
1984	85.1	63.5
1985	92.2	45.5
1986	95.6	36.5
1987	96.4	30.8
1988	97.1	26.9
1989	97.0	24.1
1990	97.2	20.9

Private Schools

Year	% with Microcomputers	Students/Computer
1983	23.8%	n.a.
1984	53.0	56.2
1985	70.3	41.6
1986	77.1	33.7
1987	78.7	28.8
1988	82.8	23.5
1989	81.8	20.1
1990	88.2	19.5

source: "Microcomputers in schools. 1986-87." Copyright 1987, Market Data Retrieval, Sheldon, Connecticut, and unpublished data by Market Data Retrieval

At the same time, the curriculum became a battleground of new teaching methods, new courses, revised texts, and competing ideologies. Meanwhile, the pressures and problems of the outside world, such as drugs, unwanted pregnancy, violence, and family turmoil, increasingly followed the students into the classrooms. Teaching—never easy—has become more difficult over the decades. Acquiring a well-rounded education and true knowledge, which always assumed diligence, requires ever more work and concentration amid the distractions and gut courses.

Here is a sampling of the busters' mixed report card, according to the National Center for Education Statistics:

• The high school graduation rate for persons aged 25 to 29 increased 15 percentage points between 1965 and 1977, to 85 percent—a record high. But it's been stuck at 85 to 86 percent ever since.

• Reading proficiency, which is vital to educational achievement, has improved modestly since 1971. But in 1988, among 17-year-olds, no racial or ethnic group read at the adept or advanced level, although whites were very close to the adept level.

• Students simply do not read enough in and out of the classroom. Frequency of library use now decreases as grade level increases. Two-thirds of 4th graders said they used the library at least weekly in 1990, compared with 25 percent of 8th graders and only 10 percent of 12th graders. Thirty percent of seniors admitted they never read for fun in their spare time.

• Science proficiency of high school seniors has improved in recent years but remains well below where it was in the early 1970s. Math skills for preteens have improved somewhat since the early 1970s, but scores for 17-year-olds overall showed no improvement. Blacks and Hispanics, however, have narrowed the math gap somewhat with whites. American students still score poorly in comparisons with math students from other developed countries.

• Thirteen percent of high school seniors were unable to identify Canada on a world map in a 1988 national survey; 15 percent didn't know where the Soviet Union was. Over one-third of seniors never took a geography course in high school.

53

• Although the gap between whites and minorities has narrowed, progress among minorities has been uneven. Ground has been lost in certain areas and gained in others.

- The share of high school seniors who reported ever using illicit drugs increased from 55 percent in 1975 to 66 percent by 1981, then fell to 44 percent by 1991. The percentage who reported drinking alcohol in the previous month rose from 68 percent in 1975 to 72 percent in 1980, then fell to 54 percent by 1991.

- Average combined scores on SAT college-entrance exams peaked at 980 in 1963, then declined steadily, bottoming out at 890 in 1980. Scores have bobbed around the 900 to 905 range in the last several years.

- More baby busters made the honor roll than did baby boomers, which reflects grade inflation and courses being "dumbed down" more than it does a genuine rise in academic achievement.

- Despite the lost ground, annual K–12 public school expenditures per pupil have risen from $2,985 in 1970 to $5,470 (in constant 1992 dollars).

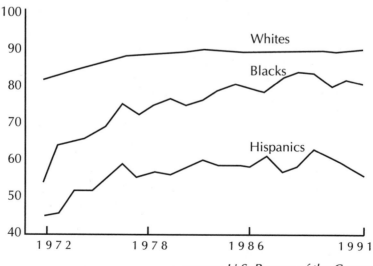

RISING EDUCATIONAL ATTAINMENT

Percent of 25-to-29-year-olds who have completed 12 or more years of school, by race

source: U.S. Bureau of the Census

The 1983 presidential report "A Nation at Risk" warned: "The educational foundations of our society are presently being eroded by a rising tide of mediocrity that threatens our very future as a nation and a people." The proportion of students who said "an important" or "very important" reason for going to college was "to improve my reading and study skills" nearly doubled between 1971 and 1990, to 43 percent, according to *The American Freshman: Twenty-Five Year Trends.* That study is a compilation of results of an ongoing survey conducted by the Higher Education Research Institute at the University of California, Los Angeles. The share who thought they may need "tutoring in specific courses" doubled between 1976 and 1990, to 16 percent. The annual survey is based on a sample of 250,000 college freshmen.

Curiously, the same surveys find that students' estimation of their own abilities has risen, which may be the result of grade inflation. In the late 1960s, there were twice as many C students as A students in high school, according to *The American Freshman.* By the 1970s and 1980s, the ratio was reversed. In 1991, 24 percent of college freshmen had a high school average of A. That's an all-time high and compares with 13 percent in 1969.

While there are more distractions in and outside the classroom that inhibit learning, another complicating factor is the growing language barrier of many students. Immigration has increased in recent decades, which means that a growing share of students are newcomers. In the unified public school district of San Jose, for example, students speak 50 different languages, making the difficult job of teaching even tougher. One-fourth of the 7,700 high school students have limited or no fluency in English. The proportions are just as high in places like Los Angeles and New York City.

But this isn't just an urban problem. In the public schools of suburban Arlington, Virginia, students speak 59 different languages, including Farsi and Khmer. Seventeen percent of Arlington's students are enrolled in ESL (English as a Second Language) programs. Even in rural Worthington, Minnesota, which has had an influx of Asian refugees in recent years, some 150 out of 2,500 students take ESL instruction. Nationwide, 5 percent of K–12 students are classified as having "limited English proficiency," according to a 1990 U.S. Department of Education survey.

55

Amid the distractions and disappointments, computers become increasingly important and can actually improve performance in other subjects and raise the level of education. While the promise of computers has not been fully realized, the progress is real, and perhaps surprising, considering that it has come during a difficult and complicated era for America's elementary and secondary schools and students. The educational report card for America's busters is, at best, mixed. But their experience with computers might be one of the brighter spots in their future.

Buster Biz

Opportunities for Buster Business

- **COMPUTERESE.** Even with computers in almost every classroom in the country, millions of baby-bust students still lack their own PCs. This is fertile ground for computer companies and outlets to plow in selling hardware and software to beginners playing catchup, as well as schools needing more and better equipment.

- **BUSTER BYTEMASTERS.** Just because many busters already have the latest computer gear and software doesn't mean that they won't need more. In fact, "computer gherkins," as young computer wizards are called by some, are a prime target for each succeeding generation of hardware and software. They're forever trading up to expand their horizons and stay on top.

- **COMPUTER TUTOR.** Those left behind in the computer revolution so far must catch up if they are to have a shot at high-paying jobs in the 1990s and beyond. It's not too late, but they'll need remedial help and user-friendly hardware and software. Designers, sales reps, educators, and employers should coordinate efforts to bring novices up to speed.

- **COMPUTER EXCHANGE.** One hacker's antique computer or a business's outdated hardware is a novice's more-than-adequate starter model, and affordable, too. As the pace of technological advances quickens, there will be an increasing supply of serviceable computers. Instead of being scrapped or shelved, these computers could easily be put back in circulation by brokers, selling them to beginners.

- **JOINING THE REVOLUTION.** The computer revolution has come to the supermarket checkout line and fast-food restaurants, where cash registers are now computerized and cashiers must know the basics of operating them. As heavy manufacturing jobs decline, there are fewer traditional blue-collar opportunities for high school graduates. They can find good work, 'new-collar' jobs in servicing and repairing computers and in data entry–if they master the computer basics. Trade schools and vocational centers must revamp their courses and faculty to meet the demand from employers and young people.

CHAPTER SIX

School Days

Baby busters are being aggressively recruited by colleges, and a larger share are going on to higher education than did baby boomers. Busters are also sticking around campus longer—much longer.

Megan Rossmann took her first PSAT test—with a #2 pencil and all those boxes to fill in—during the spring of her sophomore year of high school, as many college-bound students routinely do. The recruitment brochures from colleges started arriving soon after. "There'd be at least three things in the mail every day for a while. By now, I've gotten about 100 probably," says Megan, a senior with a B average and College Board SAT scores that are above average. "There were a lot of little schools you've never heard of."

One evening each fall, a few miles from Megan's home in the Washington, D.C. suburb of Centreville, Virginia, the Fair Oaks Mall hosts recruiters from several hundred colleges and universities who talk up their schools with local teens who wander by. And there are usually recruiters from three or four different colleges visiting the career center at Megan's high school each week.

"I think a lot of it is that there's not as many of us as there were of the baby boomers. And I think a lot of them need the money, because they're making a lot of budget cuts at the state schools," theorizes Megan, who's narrowed her choices to ten schools, including Auburn.

Auburn, a public university in Alabama, offered her a conditional acceptance while she was only a junior, based on SAT test scores of 1,000 and her B average from a public high school known to be competitive.

"I don't recall nearly the competition ... I just don't remember the pressure. It was, 'Yeah, you're going to go. Where are you going to go?' But it wasn't intense like this," says Megan's mother, Michele Rossmann, 43, remembering her own college days in Illinois during the baby-boom era.

While boomer students were competing with one another for desk space in overcrowded classrooms, today's colleges are competing with each other to fill up desks from a smaller pool of teenagers. Advantage: buster.

In addition to inundating high schoolers with recruitment literature, colleges are also sending personal letters and videotapes to names on mailing lists made available by standardized testing services and other sources. Recruiters and alumni are also making house calls. The efforts are directed at parents, as well as their children.

"Colleges have been much more pro-active in recent years as the number of traditional [high school] graduates has declined," says Wayne Becraft, executive director of the American Association of Collegiate Registrars and Admissions Officers. "They've gone to advertising in the media, which previously many institutions did not do—more direct mail, videotapes, telephone contact from the institution—a number of ways that are beyond the more traditional methods of high school visitations and college fairs."

While elite schools like Harvard, Princeton, and Yale are still turning many applicants away, smaller private colleges without large endowments and alumni networks have become particularly aggressive in their recruitment to stay alive. Dozens have gone under in the last few decades, too slow or unable to respond to the challenge posed by the baby bust. Public universities, which have their state legislatures to turn to for funding and the appeal of comparatively lower tuitions, have nevertheless gotten more aggressive, too, amid funding cutbacks.

THE STEADY DROP IN THE POOL OF 18-TO-21-YEAR-OLDS

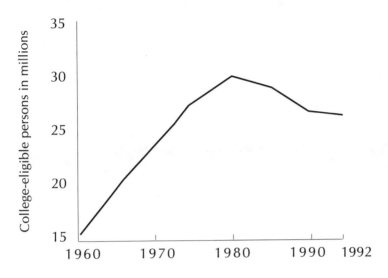

source: U.S. Bureau of the Census

"Schools are reaching farther than they used to to attract students," notes Becraft. "Public schools that may have recruited in the past just in their own state are now reaching further. The University of Maryland might recruit heavily in Pennsylvania, Virginia, maybe the New York area. Florida schools recruit in New York because they draw heavily from that area. A number of schools are also recruiting internationally."

The strong appeal of state universities is the tuition and board that run 25 to 30 percent less than at private universities. In an era when elite and even second-tier universities can cost $20,000 a year, a growing number of students are choosing public universities, in-state and out.

Making the Grade

Busters are not merely wanted; they are coveted and courted by colleges frantic to fill desks and dormitory space. Schools that have closed are evidence of the power of busters and the risk of ignoring them.

While the baby bust has contributed to dozens of colleges going out of business, overall college enrollment has actually risen slightly, to a record 14.3 million students in the 1992–93 school year, despite forecasts of a free-fall. "A lot of that is due to the increasing enrollment of women and older students, and more part-time students," explains Vance Grant, a trends analyst at the U.S. Department of Education. By 1989, 41 percent of all college students were older than 25, up from 25 percent in 1976. At the same time, higher proportions of high school students are now going to college. By 1991, a record-high 62 percent of June high school graduates enrolled in college that fall, up from 49 percent in 1980 and 45 percent in 1960.

COLLEGE-BOUND HIGH SCHOOL GRADS

Percent of eligible high school graduates who attend some college.

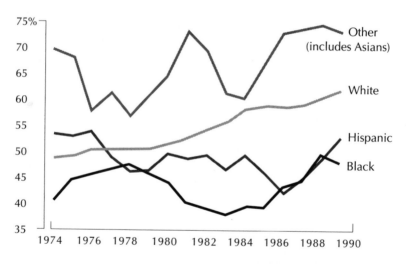

source: *U.S. Bureau of the Census*

The proportion of women enrolling in college is the highest it has ever been, 67 percent—9 points higher than for men. This means that colleges have to pay attention to women. The highly rated Rose-Hulman Institute of Technology in Terre Haute, Indiana, for example, is determined to keep up its enrollments and stiff admission standards. But realizing the changes in society caused by the needs and wants of busters, the traditionally all-male school will go coed in 1995.

Of all groups, Asian Americans have the highest level of educational attainment by far on most measures. Of the oldest baby busters, 92 percent of Asians completed high school on time, compared with 85 percent of non-Hispanic whites, 78 percent of blacks, and 72 percent of Hispanics.

Asian students averaged 530 on their math SAT scores in 1991, the only ones to crack the 500-point barrier; non-Hispanic whites averaged 489; Mexican-Americans, 427; Puerto Ricans, 406; other Hispanics, 431; and blacks, 385. On the verbal SATs, whites on average scored highest, 441; followed by Asians, 411; Hispanics in the mid-to-high 300s; blacks, 351.

Each year since 1986, over 70 percent of Asian-American high school graduates have enrolled in college that fall. The comparable 1989 rates for other groups were whites, 62 percent; Hispanics, 53 percent, and blacks, 48 percent. Hispanics, however, are less likely than blacks or whites to complete high school.

Asian Americans represent 4.4 percent of 1991 total college enrollment, which is higher than their 2.9 percent of the population. In contrast, blacks, Hispanics, and American Indians are somewhat underrepresented in college, at 9.3 percent, 6.0 percent, and 0.8 percent, respectively. Non-Hispanic whites comprise 76.5 percent of college students. The balance, 2.9 percent, are foreign students of various races. Since 1976, the minority percentage in colleges has increased, particularly for Asians and Hispanics, as enrollment has grown more diverse. The black percentage, after declining somewhat during the 1980s, is approaching the 1976 peak of 9.7 percent.

"Minority students make up a higher proportion of the student body at two-year than at four-year institutions and at public than at private institutions," according to *The Condition of Education 1992*, published by the National Center for Education Statistics.

And while the achievement of Asians is remarkable, there is a flip side. Twenty percent of Asian Americans over age 25 have less than a high school diploma, a rate higher than for non-Hispanic whites, which reflects the diversity of the Asian population and the significant influx of immigrants, particularly refugees, with little formal education.

63

While blacks and Hispanics continue to lag well behind Asians and whites, there has been significant progress in the last three decades in several—but not all—areas. And the gap has narrowed, although progress slowed or stalled during the 1980s.

The share of blacks aged 25 to 29 who have completed four or more years of high school has risen from 54 percent in 1971 to 84 percent by 1987, dipping to 81 percent by 1991. Forty-five percent of Hispanics in the same age group had completed four or more years of high school in 1971. The proportion was 63 percent in 1988 and 56 percent in 1991. The comparable figure for whites in 1991 was 90 percent. No figures are available for Asians.

Perhaps one of the most striking and heartening statistics is that there are now 2 million black college graduates in America, an increase of 1,600 percent since 1950.

While one could argue with what's being taught to young people today—and many do—a higher percentage overall are enrolled in post-secondary education than ever before.

Serious, Studious, But in No Hurry

The level of overall educational attainment has also been rising. Busters may yet wrest the title of best-educated generation from the baby boomers, who were far more educated than any previous generation.

"Almost to a person, [students are] here because they're thinking about their job afterwards," says William Vehse, provost at West Virginia University. "Twenty years ago or so was the Vietnam era, and we saw a lot of political activism. We don't see that much anymore."

The average college student now takes almost 6 years to finish college, compared with 4.5 years in 1972, and a little over 4 years in the 1960s. While men seeking student deferments from the draft boosted enrollment during the Vietnam era, they completed college in the standard 4 years, because to drop out meant to be reclassified as 1A, eligible for the draft.

With no draft to worry about, younger boomers and busters have been taking longer to finish school. Busters especially are taking lighter loads, stretching college out. That's just fine with the colleges and universities who keep the same students sitting at their desks that much longer.

"I feel like everyone doesn't know what to do. Me and a lot of my friends are like 'what are we supposed to do? Well, what do I want to do?' There are so many things out there. You have to make a choice. And so many people are staying in college longer, or waiting, because they don't know what to do or where the future's going to go."

—Deborah Morrison, 25, Morgantown, West Virginia

Many busters drop in and out of school, and back in again, changing their major a few times, often combining college with an assortment of jobs.

Contrary to appearances, busters are not wasting their time or shirking responsibility. Rather, they're sampling what's out there, proceeding cautiously, fully aware of the big stakes involved. They might also be reacting to what they perceive as the mistakes and excesses of their boomer brothers and sisters and aunts and uncles.

"Move out, move in. Start school, stop school. Get a job, quit a job. Get married, get divorced. Young adults go back and forth like boomerangs," wrote Martha Farnsworth Riche in the May 1990 issue of *American Demographics*. "It's not because they're spoiled or rebellious. It's because young adults face increasingly complex choices; they must investigate more options before they can settle into adult life. Boomeranging is a rational response to changes in our society and economy. It is here to stay."

65

Between being adolescents and grownups, busters have developed a new stage in the life cycle, which Riche calls "pre-adults." It's sort of an adulthood apprenticeship; and it's not so bad. They are gaining valuable job experience, which theoretically should put them in a better position to make a serious career decision at the appropriate time. And while they may bounce from job to job at the mall, busters are building up their savings—and disposable income. Since busters are waiting longer to marry, they have more to spend on themselves during their teens and 20s. The things that young Americans are buying now, other than pizza and beer, include many big-ticket items: cars, motorcycles, cameras, computers, electronic equipment, recreational gear, clothes, and airline tickets.

Although anxious parents may be puzzled by the habits of their offspring, this elongated state of pre-adulthood should become as popular with marketers searching for new targets as it is with young adults not wanting to rush things and college presidents eager to fill desks and dorm space.

Buster Biz

Opportunities for Buster Business

- **HELP!** True, colleges are breaking the backs of mail carriers and burning up the telephone lines to lure busters to their schools. But once they land on campus, many need remedial help, which opens opportunities for tutoring services as well as publishers and bookstores specializing in remedial texts and self-improvement and guide books.

- **MONEY, MONEY, MONEY.** Money, indeed, is what students need and what local bankers can provide lots of, at fair market interest, to pay for rising tuition and expenses during times of cutbacks in college and government grants.

- **PLASTIC.** Sixty percent of collegians now have credit cards. They're primed to charge and use ATMs. Local bankers and merchants should get their charge cards into the hands of incoming freshmen, assuming their credit is good.

- **GET A JOB.** To help pay for tuition and credit charges, a majority of busters will work during their college years, providing a motivated labor force to employers near campus.

- **STIMULATING THE ECONOMY.** They have the rest of their lives to save. Right now, busters are determined to spend on jeans, trendy jackets, T-shirts and sweatshirts with logos and rad sayings, computers, VCRs, cameras, video games, sports gear, pizza, beer, and hamburgers. Merchants, stock accordingly. And make sure the wrapping is biodegradable. These customers check.

- **FILL 'ER UP.** Since a growing number of buster scholars are living at home and commuting to community colleges to cut costs, they'll need wheels—new or used—and gas to get to and from class.

- **TAKE YOUR TIME.** While they are fewer than the boomers, busters are taking almost two years longer to finish college. That almost counterbalances their smaller numbers and means they'll be around campus nearly six years, spending on goods and services.

CHAPTER SEVEN

The Buster Work Force

A shrinking labor pool has not always meant easy employment for baby busters, who are often over-qualified for available jobs. But there's hope for busters with the right skills.

The help-wanted ad in the newspaper industry trade magazine *Editor & Publisher*, read: "Ambitious but stuck behind a bunch of baby boomers at a major metro? Eager for greater responsibility and a chance to advance? We're looking for you." The ad could have been written by a psychiatrist specializing in the buster psyche. It touched all the right buttons: boomer distrust, career angst, plus a desire to be heard, taken seriously, and appreciated.

The experience of busters in the work force thus far has been decidedly mixed. "I feel like I've been part of a depression," says Lizabeth MacDonald, a 1992 college graduate who spent eight months interviewing for an entry-level staff position on Capitol Hill.

She landed a spot as an aide to a congressional committee, but it fell through at the last minute. To get experience and job leads, she then volunteered in a congressional office. To pay the bills, she worked nights for $6 an hour as a telephone fundraiser for an environmental organization for a while, and then as a manager at a trendy pizzeria at Union Station in Washington, D.C. All the while, she flooded congressional offices with her resumé, which included a Capitol Hill internship during her junior year of college. The resumé she submitted in red envelopes with candy canes attached drew attention and generated interviews. One eventually led to a paid position as a staff assistant to a newly elected representative from California. "Now I realize that everything is not handed to you just because you have a degree," says MacDonald, 23. "The timelines have changed. Now it can take a good 6, 8, maybe even 12 months to get the first real job. You have to go out and find the opportunities, whereas my parents and even the baby boomers, it took maybe a month or 2."

Quips her housemate Tracy Birkhahn: "I think we start in the basement, then work to the bottom." Birkhahn, 23, spent most of the summer of 1992 job hunting before securing a junior position on a senatorial staff. "The job openings were totally sparse. I did what I could. And it was really luck is all—being in the right place at the right time."

MacDonald, Birkhahn, and two other buster housemates, all recent college graduates drawn to Washington, D.C., discuss the facts of life in the labor force of the 1990s. "I just feel I'm almost in this brain drain, because it's not like my mind is being put to good use," says Tamara Russell, 23. Despite getting a job as a staff assistant on Capitol Hill, the work so far has been mostly clerical and menial. She wonders if intense competition hasn't caused older workers to be stuck in entry-level positions, thus becoming her direct competitors. "I just hope that some day: (a), I'm happy with my life, and (b) I have a job where I'm really satisfied," she says.

Housemate Holly Woung, 24, is working as a receptionist in a law firm that wanted a college graduate for the position. "It's not really what I want to be, but I needed a job and I took it," she says. "It doesn't take too long to realize that you're not using your brain and it's not the place to be." Woung plans to go to graduate school to prepare for a career as a teacher or school administrator.

The talk among many busters across the country reveals an undercurrent of worry about career prospects, no doubt fueled by the protracted recession and corporate layoffs of the early 1990s, the subsequent slow, uneven recovery, as well as the confusing, contradictory comments of allegedly expert economists and media pundits.

In 1991, with a U.S. jobless rate of 6.7 percent, the rate for 18- and 19-year-olds stood at 17 percent, and 11 percent for 20-to-24-year-olds, according to the Bureau of Labor Statistics. It dropped to 6.8 percent for those aged 25 to 34.

"I see so many people pay all this money and spend all this time, four years of college, and come out and work at Taco Bell. They got a degree and everything, but they can't get a job," says Jim McFadden, a buster who grew up in southern California. "So, I figured I might as well get a trade, you know, something to fall back on." For the past nine years, McFadden has been a diesel mechanic, specializing in maintaining and repairing Caterpillar heavy machinery. He's been back to trade school several times to upgrade his skills to stay current with the newer machinery that comes loaded with electronic gear.

McFadden works hard and long hours, but he's well paid and his job is secure, because he smartly picked a trade that's in demand in his particular labor market. At age 28, he and his wife Bridget, who is a receptionist, own their own two-bedroom home in Moreno Valley. "I just think that everybody needs to educate themselves as much as possible. You've got to work more with your mind than with your back. Because if you think you're going to make it with your back, you're going to lose out," McFadden contends. "You've got to just educate yourself about life and whatever trade you're going into, because it's tough out there."

McFadden is correct on every point. In the 1990s and beyond, whether hunting for a white-collar or blue-collar job, prospective employers will increasingly place a premium on education and skills. In the Bureau of Labor Statistics' 1991 report on job projections to the year 2005, Associate Commissioner Ronald E. Kutscher writes: "Those jobs growing the fastest currently are filled by workers with higher levels of education. This clearly does not mean that everyone must have a four-year college degree to find a job. But it does point out that an increasingly important opportunity difference is emerging along the lines of educational preparation."

• VOX BUSTER •

"The problem is that when baby boomers graduated from college, they were considered to be educated. When baby busters graduate from college, we are considered unskilled and marginally employable. So what we have is a generation of people—baby busters with college educations—who are treated as if they lack skills by their employers who are often times baby boomers with the same level of education. The rules are continually changing: we are forced to jump through changing, meaningless, and insulting hoops. As soon as we jump through one, they put another one in front of us. I see baby boomers who have bachelor's degrees and have worked their way up the ladder of their organizations. When resumés come across their desks for an entry-level researcher, let's say, they won't consider those without Ph.D. written on them. One thing I often hear is that my generation should feel grateful to have the opportunity to be underpaid and work in jobs for which we are overqualified. I'm tired of xeroxing for hypocritical baby boomers and tired of being stepped on by bleeding ponytails."

—Heather Francese, 28, Washington, D.C.

The Early Years

Some background: A decade ago and long before the recession, the comparatively small size of the baby bust began triggering serious labor shortages as older busters started entering the work force. The first shortages occurred in retail, particularly the fast-food industry, which traditionally relies heavily on young entry-level workers.

As McDonald's and its rivals opened new restaurants and malls kept springing up, employers had an increasingly tough time finding enough young people to wait on customers during what was an economic boom. The 1980s—the Reagan years and the beginning of the Bush administration—were the country's longest period of sustained economic growth. During the 1980s, some 19 million new jobs were created. That only increased the need for young workers, who were too few in number to fill all the entry-level openings.

In 1972, with the leading edge of the baby boom well into the labor force, workers under age 25 accounted for 23 percent of the labor force, according to the Bureau of Labor Statistics. By 1986, only 20 percent of the labor force was under age 25. The BLS projects the proportion will drop to 16 percent by the year 2000.

WHERE ARE THE (YOUNG) WORKERS GOING?

16-to-24-year-olds as a percentage of the American work force.

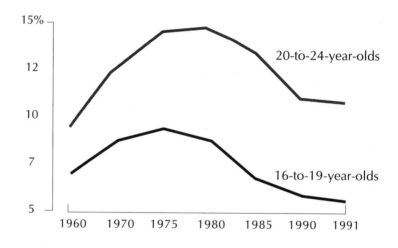

source: *U.S. Bureau of Labor Statistics*

In a 1987 white paper, then Assistant Labor Secretary Roger D. Semerad cautioned employers: "As a result of a diminished rate of labor force growth and a smaller pool of qualified workers, particularly at the entry level, some employers may face skill shortages.

"Employers could respond to this situation by exporting jobs overseas, bidding up wages for qualified workers, investing more heavily in automation, or spending more for training and education of new employees."

Burger King, for example, redesigned its restaurants' layout and machinery to boost productivity and cut the actual steps workers must take to complete an order. At many of its locations, Arby's has introduced the Touch 2000 computer system, which lets customers place their orders by touching the appropriate items displayed on the screen. The system has cut order time to 45 seconds from the pre-Touch 2000 average of 100 seconds. Four workers can now handle eight lines of customers; before, it took eight workers to run four lines.

As employers grew desperate for entry-level workers, help-wanted signs became a permanent fixture in shop windows; starting salaries rose; workers received bonuses to recruit friends; and more seniors and handicapped people were hired. "Baby busters can afford to be picky with colleges and jobs," asserted *The Numbers News* in its April 1988 issue. "Just as the baby boom competed for jobs, employers are now competing for young workers."

Diane Crispell, editor of *TheNumbers News*, added: "Employers have been facing a shortage of young workers for some years now, ever since the first buster turned 16 in 1981. Baby boomers were grateful for minimum-wage jobs in fast-food restaurants in their teen years. Those same restaurants are now paying baby busters close to twice the minimum wage in some places and are still having trouble filling positions. Employers of entry-level workers have resorted to recruiting housewives and retired people to fill the gap left by the baby bust."

Throughout the 1980s, busters had more jobs to choose from, less competition from one another, and advanced more quickly than did baby boomers at the same stage in their lives. The rapid job growth came in the services, a broad category that stretches from high-tech to sales and service of various types. Many of the new sales and service jobs were low-paying, such as hamburger flippers and counter sales personnel at malls. But other new jobs paid quite well: computer sales, financial planning, and Wall Street bond traders.

There has emerged in the vast service sector and the amorphous information industry what some have called "new-collar" jobs: nonunion but fairly good-paying and reasonably secure, skilled jobs, often in the suburbs and tied to computers. Such jobs include computer programmers, information specialists who work by telephone, overnight delivery handlers, and assorted installers and repairers of computer, electronic, and copier equipment.

Shortages of busters were severest in the major metro areas of the Northeast, which during most of the 1980s had a robust economy and the lowest unemployment in the country. Exacerbating the baby-bust problem were historically high housing and living costs in places like New York City, Fairfield County in Connecticut, and northern New Jersey, which forced many young people to move away or to move back in with Mom and Pop.

Despite an influx of high-paying Fortune 500 companies to Fairfield County, the area had a chronic shortage of clerks, secretaries, administrative assistants, and junior executives. Similar shortages were noted in Westchester County, New York, and parts of Morris, Essex, Somerset, and Hunterdon counties in suburban New Jersey.

Don't Call Us, We'll Call You—*NOT!*

The buster advantage decreased—at least temporarily—in the 1990–91 recession and slow recovery. After a decade of hiring and expansion, companies large and small started laying people off in the late 1980s in the wake of the S&L mess, the stock market and real-estate slump, and stiffening competition from overseas. U.S. unemployment, which had been at 5.3 percent in 1989, rose to 6.7 percent in 1991, and reached 7.4 percent in 1992.

Even as they needed more competent and better-trained workers to compete more effectively, many companies cut back on training programs. Busters entering the labor force were suddenly competing for jobs with older laid-off workers, many of them boomers.

Buster Dan Holland, a 1991 graduate of the highly regarded Carnegie Mellon University in Pittsburgh, with an impressive resumé, worked several months with one Pittsburgh museum on a preservation project until its completion.

In fall 1992, he moved to Austin, Texas, with the hope of landing a job with another preservation project. After a few months of working days as a telemarketer for an Austin newspaper and nights as a waiter to pay the rent, he decided to move back East to pursue job leads. He worked briefly as a research assistant in a Pittsburgh law firm while living with his parents. But by early 1993, he had landed a job as a research assistant for a trade association in Arlington, Virginia, a position more to his liking, but requiring his third move in four months.

His time in Austin was a rude awakening. "A lot of the people—a little bit older than us—are fighting for their lives, because they're the ones who lost a lot of jobs. They're the ones who are probably going to get those back," says Holland.

"I was hired for the telemarketing job, along with another guy my age and this woman who's at least in her 50s. She said she had just been laid off. She had been working at this big firm for 14 years. What's the only job available? These low- to mid-wage jobs. I've worked in several restaurants where people are married and have kids.

"So, it's going to be extremely competitive. And I think our generation is not taking advantage of the amount of time and the amount of information we have available to us. A lot of people have been intimidated by the recession."

The long-term marketplace prospects for busters are a matter of debate and confusion among demographers, economists, busters, and bosses. "To the Class of '92: Why Not Try Med School?" ran the attention-grabbing headline on a June 1, 1992 article in *Advertising Age* about job prospects in the ad industry. "The contraction of the advertising business continues, and high levels of unemployment mean newcomers with little or no experience will find job opportunities particularly slim in 1992," writes senior reporter Gary Levin.

Interestingly though, the comments from the ten leading ad executives quoted were not uniformly grim and discouraging. While some advised against advertising, others offered cautious encouragement. "I think it's the best time to do it because we need new blood in this business ... There's always an opening for a young, new, promising advertising person," contends Philip Dusenberry, vice chairman of BBDO Worldwide.

"I think it's an opportune time. There are few jobs, but there are always few jobs," said Stephen O. Frankfurt, chairman of Frankfurt Gips Balkind. "We're in such a state of change that the opportunity is tremendous. Most of our people are very young; they bring fresh ideas. I'd go for it and do anything I could to get in."

Even in the protracted recession of the early 1990s, there were some surprising labor shortages, which only points up the complexity of the economy and the need for job-seekers to track trends closely and go where the work is. As Eric Schmitt reported in the September 12, 1992 *New York Times*: "At a time when the Pentagon is actually paying people to leave the service, the military is having trouble signing up tens of thousands of new troops, in part because of the overwhelming perception that new recruits are not needed or wanted.

"Not so, military officials say. While they are thinning out the middle and higher ranks for a smaller, post-Cold War force, the Army, Navy, Air Force, and Marine Corps still need recruits to ensure that the armed forces are properly proportioned for the future.

"Indeed, the Army alone is aiming to bring in 85,000 new enlisted troops next year; right now it is about 10 percent behind in the number of recruits it has signed up."

In any field, the busters' strength is the strength that newcomers to the work force have always had: youth, adaptability, lower wage demands, and a hunger to get established, in contrast to senior workers, who are slowing down, set in their ways, and at the top of the wage scale.

The 1990–91 recession, as with all recessions, was a correction of the overproduction that preceded it. But as people temporarily cut back on their consumption, there inevitably builds a pent-up demand for goods and services, to be followed by rising sales, employment, and hiring. At the same time, there is an ongoing restructuring of the U.S. economy as it continues its shift from heavy manufacturing to services. With the recovery underway, downsized companies are cautiously hiring again. This boosts prospects for qualified busters, even if their prospects are not currently as bright as they were in pre-recession days.

In 1993, busters are aged 17 to 28. As they advance through their careers, they will represent a smaller pool of workers at each rung than the ones that preceded them. Economist Richard A. Easterlin is one who sees bright job prospects for busters, because of their relatively small size and scarcity in the work force. In this sense, busters are like the Depression generation that entered the work force in the 1940s and 1950s. In his provocative book, *Birth and Fortune: The Impact of Numbers on Personal Welfare*, Easterlin argues: "As we move into the late 1980s and 1990s, those born in the recent low-birth-rate era will increasingly find, as they reach the labor market, that job openings are plentiful, wage rates relatively good, and advancement rapid. Their incomes will rise relative to older workers, and the unemployment rate among younger workers will fall. This, combined with the shrinking percentage of younger workers in the labor force, will lower the national unemployment rate and will ease inflationary pressures. The more favorable economic environment generally will reinforce the feelings of economic security that young adults are developing because of their favorable labor market experience. They will find it easier to satisfy their economic aspirations and to play their expected roles in life. Psychological stress will be reduced, and feelings of hopelessness or bitterness will be less prevalent."

Easterlin admits in his book: "Although my view of the next 20 years is in the minority, I have some company on a few particulars. Economists Joseph M. Anderson, Michael L. Wachter, and Finis Welch separately argue that the growing scarcity of young adults in the next decade should result in a substantial improvement in their relative earnings and in a reduction in their unemployment rates."

CAUTION: Wide Load Ahead—Stalled Boomers

On the other hand, Wall Street analyst Dick Hokenson, research vice-president of Donaldson, Lufkin & Jenrette Securities Corporation, contends that busters' comparatively small size will really only benefit busters in the early years of their careers. "If you looked at the organizational charts of most companies, it's probably easier for the post-boom generation to get the first or second job, first and maybe second promotion," he says.

Hokenson, an economic demographer who writes a newsletter that analyzes demographic trends for their investment implications, adds: "But then the problem in many companies is that basically they're just staring at the heels of the baby boom. That's what I think gives them some greater sense of downward mobility."

The sheer size of the baby-boom generation has caused the career advancement of many boomers to slow, if not stall, at a middle rung. As the organizational pyramid gets narrower with each higher rung, there is just not enough room at the top to handle all the boomers. To address the potential problems of slumping morale and productivity, companies are offering what are euphemistically called lateral promotions—new assignments, better titles, but at the same management and pay level—to keep talented people challenged and reasonably happy. Employers are also offering new benefits in lieu of pay raises: flex-time, day care, fitness and health facilities, assorted self-improvement and job-related courses, part-time teaching and mentoring opportunities, and sabbaticals. Not surprisingly, some stalled boomers are jumping ship; others are being pushed, which opens up the pipeline for younger busters.

The boomer logjam is not uniform across the board. "There are not nearly enough people with college degrees or advanced vocational and technical training to fill the more than 2 million new managerial, administrative, and technical jobs coming online annually," contend John Naisbitt and Patricia Aburdene in their 1990 book *Megatrends 2000.*

Alan Reynolds, director of economic research at the Hudson Institute, is among those most enthusiastic about the prospects for busters. Dismissing naysayers and undaunted by the 1990–91 recession, Reynolds observed in a 1992 op-ed piece in the *Washington Times*: "In the 1990s, demographics alone are certain to push real wages and salaries way up, even if economic growth remains slow (which is quite unlikely in this exciting era of accelerating technological marvels). The baby boom has busted, and that means there will be very few young people seeking jobs. Even unskilled labor will be relatively scarce, and skilled and energetic labor will be in strong demand all over the world. Employers faced with such tight labor markets have no choice but to pay attractive salaries if they hope to attract and retain good workers. ...

"Far from having a harder time than their parents, those in their teens and 20s right now are going to find it much easier to get real pay increases than their parents did. Since current young people also start out in an economy with a large stock of modern capital equipment, and without the chronic inflation of housing costs, their rapid pay increases will also go much further."

Where Jobs Will Be in the 21st Century

Between 1990 and 2005, jobs are projected to increase by 25 million, according to the Bureau of Labor Statistics' (BLS) moderate forecast series. That growth compares with an increase of 34.9 million between 1975 and 1990. The annual increase is projected at 1.2 percent between 1990 and 2005, which is half the rate of the previous 15 years.

The service sector will contribute 23 million of the 25 million new jobs. Health services and business services alone are expected to account for 6.1 million. The BLS expects the ten fastest-growing industries to be, in descending order: residential care, computer and data processing services, health services, management and public relations, water and sanitation, libraries/vocational and other schools, offices of health practitioners, passenger transportation arrangements, social services, and legal services. Jobs in those industries will grow at two to four times the national rate.

• VOX BUSTER •

"I wouldn't say the outlook is just magnificent. I wouldn't say it's bad. But I wouldn't say it all looks great."

—Jason Palmer, 21, Weatherford, Oklahoma

The U.S. Department of Education has estimated that 30 percent of new jobs created during the 1990s will require a college degree, up from 22 percent a decade ago. Even those not requiring degrees will require increasing schooling and training.

"The new generation has set the mold as far as having an education and training. You just have to. Whereas in the baby-boom era, they walked into jobs and learned on the job," contends Catherine Coleman, 28. A college graduate, she is a housing advisor with the Fair Housing Center in greater Chicago.

In his first job as a youth counselor in his hometown of Newark, New Jersey, Leland Brown recalls: "I have no experience and no college degree. I had nothing but my military experience, which, as far as child care was concerned, was nothing. I started in December 1988. The next month, they made it a requirement that you have a minimum of a two-year degree or prior experience in the field. That shows there is a trend toward more education or more training.

"It's not that necessary that you have a college degree, but they're looking for people who have had some experience. And this is where a lot of my generation is getting caught, because they want to start at the top. But you're not going to get anything at the top unless you have some type of experience or degree. But to get that training, you're going to have to start at the bottom."

Brown, 27, who now works for the State of New York as a counselor, enjoys his job working directly with and helping troubled youths. But he's looking ahead. He plans to take college courses in social work in hopes of one day switching into an administrative or managerial position. Not only would such a promotion mean a jump in salary, prestige, and responsibility, but it would also mean less grueling hours and emotionally draining work.

"The job market is a lot harder than 15 to 20 years ago. It'll definitely change more by the 21st century. Yeah, I think it'll affect me. I'm all for getting more skills," says Greg Phillips, 21, of Joplin, Missouri. He worked a few years at an auto garage in high school and the last three years pouring hot metal for $6 an hour at a foundry, where he makes manhole covers and grates. "The place I'm working, I don't plan on working there forever or anything."

While his lack of higher education may have closed some doors, Phillips believes there are alternative routes to success, starting with hard work. He's considering enlisting in the Army as a way to get technical training and school benefits to further develop skills marketable in the civilian world afterwards.

"If I had any choice, I'd like to go and learn how to work on computers and stuff like that." Phillips sees himself one day being a computer repairman or troubleshooter. "There's a lot of work in the hospitals and all kinds of places that have computers. I think it would be kind of neat. I like messing with electronics."

Even in the construction industry, there is growing concern about finding quality workers and the need to provide basic training for many of them. "Now, more and more, you find motivated, intelligent individuals that you simply are going to have to train," says Dick Maresco, vice president for education at Associated Builders and Contractors (ABC), a trade association representing 16,000 construction firms across the U.S.

Many ABC member firms have to teach new hires basic math and are even giving reading tests as a qualification for training. "When we start training entry-level people, they usually do not have the minimum math requirements for the construction industry. So we have basically got to train them to do it. It's been that way for at least 10 or 15 years. At one time, they did have the math skills. Our high school systems are just not doing the job," Maresco claims.

In addition to basic math, ABC's member firms offer courses in 16 trades, courses designed by ABC for helpers wanting to develop a skill and journeymen workers wanting to advance. "It's necessary because of the higher technology required and the additional safety requirements of federal regulations," says Maresco. "Buildings and roads and dams are just more difficult to build today because of higher standards. And you've got to have this training. Also the career-long training we hope will encourage additional people to stay in the construction industry and pursue opportunities."

Rosetta Tate, 28, married and the mother of three, is in the second year of a four-year training course in Baton Rouge, Louisiana, to become a journeyman electrician. She studies two nights a week, while holding down a day job as an electrician's helper.

"It's hard work, but it pays good money," says Rosetta, which is why she got into it after years as a hotel clerk. "It [hotel clerk job] paid a little over minimum wage. And we just couldn't make it on that. ... I got up one morning and decided I was tired of making minimum wage." As an electrician's helper, her income is now double what it was at the hotel. With added training, her wage scale will rise another $3 or $4 an hour. "I didn't have the chance to go to college. It's like a second chance," she says of her trade schooling.

"People are looking more to education as a way to make more money. A lot of people I know are going back to school to get more education so they can make a better check, so they can take care of their family. It's so hard out in the world making $6 and $7 an hour. If you don't have an education, you're not going to have a good job," Tate maintains.

81

During his one year at college, Scott Pitre worked part-time "pushing pizza" and bagging groceries. That year was enough to convince him that he didn't want college and he didn't want to bag groceries. "It was pretty boring and pretty dead-end," he admits. "It definitely gave me inspiration to do something to improve myself, learn a trade of some sort, get some sort of education."

Now halfway through ABC's electrical and instrumentation course, Pitre, 22, is a first-step journeyman electrician in Baton Rouge, with a high-paying job, and a secure future, if he continues to learn.

"There's just so much new technology coming along. They've got to have people adapt to it. The only way to do it is to educate them," says Pitre. And the prospect of periodically retraining doesn't scare him. "I like it. It lets me know I'm not going to be stuck doing the same thing over and over, day in and day out. I'm going to have to change. If I have to get education and be trained to do it, that's fine by me."

Of his prospects, he says: "I have very good confidence as far as what my job status will be in the future because of the older persons who are working. I'd say that a fair percentage of them aren't annually updating skills or anything and they are only going to be there for X amount of years. And then that just leaves that many more jobs for us, people my age who are being trained. They're the older guys, learned their trade on the job. They learned how to do their one thing, and they haven't learned anything new."

For tradesmen wanting to move into management, ABC in the last five years developed weeklong courses for becoming a project manager, supervisor, estimator, safety coordinator, even a construction executive. The courses, which are taught by practitioners, are offered at Clemson University in South Carolina.

What ABC is doing is being repeated by firms in other industries that are determined to upgrade the skills of their workers and keep companies and products competitive.

To the extent that busters stay in school and get training appropriate to the needs of the economy, they should be in demand again in fast-growing fields. "The relative scarcity of young people also has important implications for schools and educational institutions," writes research demographer Carol J. De Vita in *America in the Twenty-first Century: A Demographic Overview*. "As the number of entry-level workers shrinks and the competition for their labor intensifies, public schools will experience greater pressure to graduate a higher percentage of students and to provide these graduates with marketable skills.

"The need for a better-educated and more productive work force will grow during the 1990s, as industries respond to changing technologies and market competition. Policymakers will be asked to consider a variety of options to meet this need, such as investing additional resources to educate student groups that schools have not served well in the past or revising immigration policies to import needed workers with specific skills from abroad."

Gerald C. Celente, director of the Socio-Economic Research Institute, believes that busters are entering the labor force at a critical and especially difficult time, but one with opportunity for those who know how to seize it. "This new generation comes in. They wonder: 'How come the economy is not growing as fast?' This is the end of the industrial age. Every institution formed during that age: family, political institutions, religions, health care, legal institutions, business, is failing to meet the needs of 21st century society," he contends.

Busters have strengths and weaknesses. "What they have going for them is their age, their youth," says Celente, himself a baby boomer. "They are an extremely bright group. Their computer fluency is phenomenal." Yet Celente finds busters overly dependent on broadcast media for information and doing too little reading and analysis for the larger meaning of things.

"The only way people are going to recognize opportunity is to recognize the change. Busters are looking at the world through the lens of what was, rather than this is what it can be," says Celente, author of a book entitled *Trend Tracking*. "They really have to track trends to know what's going on. You have to understand the changes that are taking place each day. There is no magic to it."

Like many boomers, busters themselves may be skipping the corporate fast-track to run their own race as entrepreneurs. A 1991 Roper CollegeTrack survey of 1,200 college students found that 38 percent viewed owning their own business as an excellent way to become successful. In another survey by UCLA's Higher Education Research Institute, 42 percent of fall 1991 college freshmen said that succeeding in their own business was essential or very important. The proportion was as high as 52 percent in the mid-1980s.

83

• VOX BUSTER •

I think even though the economy is bad, it is still to our advantage for those that are energetic, for those who are go-getters. Those of us who sit and wait for something to come to us, that's all we're ever going to do, we're always going to be sitting there waiting. But for those of us who are persistent and consistent, who get up and go out there and maybe start out at the bottom of the ladder, and really work hard and hustle, there is a lot out there, because there aren't that many of us. So the competition isn't that great. So the potential to excel is greater than in the previous generation.

—Leland Brown, 27, Danbury, Connecticut

Celente says in his book: "For people seeking jobs in the 1990s, the good news is that there's going to be a labor shortage. The bad news is that at the same time there's going to be a relatively high rate of unemployment. This is because of the growing mismatch between the products of our educational system and the needs of our society. If you have an appropriate education, you'll have no trouble getting a job. If you don't have one, you'll risk being unemployed."

To students, regardless of major, Celente advises: "Be sure to learn a foreign language. Better yet, learn two foreign languages. Learn about foreign cultures, as much as you can. Whether you go into business, government, research, or the arts, your future will depend on your ability to function in the global market. So get a global education."

And for those already on the job, he writes: "Continue your education. I don't mean going to an occasional seminar or workshop, I mean applying yourself to learn new things, as much as if you were getting an advanced degree. You may actually get an advanced degree, or do the equivalent by taking courses or studying on your own. Whatever you do, you should always be getting useful information, tracking trends, and anticipating change."

84

Marketable skills and adaptability will be highly prized and essential qualifications for entry-level and experienced workers in the 1990s. College is not necessarily the answer for everyone.

While the economy continues its shift away from heavy manufacturing to high-tech and services, there will also be opportunities for accomplished tradesmen, fueled in part by the home-remodeling and expansion boom, which is fueled by baby boomers who are turning their homes into castles.

Writes Celente in *Trend Tracking*, "I'm talking about carpenters, masons, plumbers, and other people who work with their hands. I'm talking about people who make things and repair things. In fact, I don't make a distinction between a surgeon and a garage mechanic. They should both have the value system that goes with being a professional. For such professionals, there will always be jobs, since there's a real shortage of them. If you've needed a plumber lately, you know this."

Buster Biz

Opportunities for Buster Business

- **GETTA JOB.** Before the 1990–91 recession, there was actually a shortage of young workers—busters. That advantage has been lost at least temporarily during the recession and slow recovery, but may reappear when the economy kicks into high gear. Career counseling and job placement have become increasingly important to workers of all ages, especially busters, in this volatile economy, which will continue to shift into high-tech and services into the 21st century.

- **GETTA WORKER.** The challenge to employers is not to find workers—there are plenty of them, including a lot of dead wood—but to find skilled and qualified applicants. That's not so easy, and the public schools haven't been much help. Still, such workers are out there, and headhunters increasingly will match a worker to an employer's needs. Personnel will be a hot field in the 1990s and beyond.

- **JOB RETRAINING.** Thirty percent of new jobs in the 1990s will require a college degree, up from 22 percent the decade before, according to the U.S. Department of Education. And many of those that may not require a college diploma will still demand a high level of skills. Thus, trade schools and colleges will be busy providing students with the skills that will get them high-paying jobs, while upgrading the skills of workers so they can stay current with the fast-changing demands of their careers. Schooling will no longer end at age 18 or 21, but continue throughout one's life.

- **TRANSLATORS/EMISSARIES.** As the nation becomes more racially and ethnically diverse, so will the work force. Between 1990 and 2005, when the labor force grows 21 percent, Asian and Hispanic workers will increase 74 percent. Rising immigration will provide growing pools of high-tech workers, as well as low-cost, unskilled labor. These new workers could become liaisons to their old countries as well as their ethnic communities here and thus help open up new markets and labor pools for their employers. But those employers and their other workers, as well as immigrant workers, will face communications problems with one another that may require everyone to learn some words in someone else's language.

86

· **HITCHING A RIDE.** Over half of the jobs are now in suburbia. That's also where two-thirds of new jobs are springing up. With people so scattered, mass transit won't work. But private car-pooling will, especially for urbanites desperate to get to jobs in the outlying suburbs. Seeing an opportunity, Detroiter Dan Williams, Jr. launched Jobs Employment Transportation Services (JETS), a fleet of 12 passenger vans that brings Detroiters to and from suburban jobs. JETS collects fares from riders and fees from employers.

· **WORKING NINE TO FIVE—*NOT!*** Don't expect busters to be wage slaves like their parents or grandparents. Loyalty went out the office window with the massive corporate layoffs of the late 1980s and early 1990s. Busters want good jobs, good hours, good times. And with both spouses likely to be working, buster couples, like boomers before them, will have to be choosier in what they will and won't do than are single-earner households. They will all be pressed for time. This creates opportunities for restaurants, travel agencies, home delivery, and other convenience services.

CHAPTER EIGHT

Staying at Home for Now

Career uncertainties, a knack for spending, and an aversion to paying rent all conspire to cause busters to be homeward bound. More and more, they are living with Mom and Dad.

Eighteen years of hard, loving work and $124,000 is the bare minimum for a middle-income family to raise a single child these days. Add another four years and $21,116 to put that same child through a public college, or $48,668 for a private college, according to 1991 estimates. No wonder America's birth rate has plunged from the pre-inflation baby-boom average of 3.7 children per couple.

After two decades of precarious parenting in the modern era, proud mothers and fathers eagerly anticipate their child's graduation from high school and maybe college, then that first real job, and passage into adulthood. Quiet is restored to the parental home, and blood pressure drops.

Then comes the knock at the door or the unexpected phone call, and the shocking announcement. "Hi, Mom. Hi, Dad. I'm moving back home." Those eight little words have been repeated millions of times in the last decade as busters fly back to the parental nest.

Still other busters, defying the laws of gravity, are staying put in their rooms. You can't beat the rent, the stocked refrigerator, and the free maid service.

"When I first graduated from college, I figured it was a hell of a lot easier on me just to stay home," reports Dan Holland, 24. He spent his first year after college at home with his parents in Pittsburgh, while he worked at a local museum as a historical preservationist. "It was cheaper. Food and rent were paid for, but I did my own wash and my own chores. I liked it. I get along well with my parents, and everything was pretty much done for me ... I've lived on my own a little, and I know it's hard. You have to watch your budget."

After that year at home, Holland moved to Austin, Texas, in hopes of landing a research position there. But after three months, no such position had opened up, so Holland packed his bags and moved back to Pittsburgh and his parents' home.

Back where he started, he worked briefly at a restaurant, and then took a clerical position with a local law firm, while interviewing widely for a real job with career potential. He said of his home and job situation at that time: "I've been raised on imported beer and nice cars. I got to drive my parents' Honda all the time and always had everything at my disposal at home. And to leave that, it's tough. I guess I don't really know what it's like to struggle...."

"But I think a lot of people face that, too. They have nowhere to go. They don't want to struggle out on their own. Plus, it's really hard. ... To live in a decent apartment, that's several hundred dollars. I don't even know if I can afford it without two jobs."

He'll be finding out mighty soon. Four months after returning to his parental nest, he had flown the coop yet again to try his wings in Arlington, Virginia, where his diligent job search finally paid off. In January 1993, he landed a challenging, well-paying job as a research assistant with a trade association. He's monitoring federal legislation, analyzing action on Capitol Hill, and writing position papers for an association representing 16,000 construction companies. Holland is also closely monitoring his own expenses now that he's affixed his name in ink to a long-term lease on an apartment.

Still at home is Vicki Teschler, a 21-year-old dental assistant and part-time college student, who lives with her widowed mother and 18-year-old sister in Clinton Township, Michigan. "Right now, it's mostly financial reasons that keep me from going out on my own. If I had the money, I would definitely move out—not that living here is bad," says Vicki.

With three credit cards and monthly payments on a new car, she concedes: "I guess if I did have my own apartment, I probably wouldn't have the clothes that I do now. And I don't know if I'd have electricity."

While she doesn't pay rent, Vicki does run errands, grocery shops, and occasionally prepares dinner for her mother and sister. She also has her own telephone line—"that was a must."

And now that she's an adult, she finds that she has "more rights and more freedom to come and go as I please." She describes her relationship with her mother as "a mother-daughter relationship, but it's more a friendship now. It's more like I'm her best friend."

Within the next two years, Vicki's hoping to get her own place. In the meantime, she's got a hope chest, which she's filling with occasional purchases—towels, silverware, and china—for when she is on her own. "I just like to relax and go with the flow," she says.

You Can Go Home Again

In 1992, a record 13.2 million persons aged 18 to 24 were living at home with their parents—54 percent—up from 11 million, or 47 percent in 1970. Twelve percent of adults aged 25 to 34 lived with their parents in 1992. Two decades before, only 8 percent did.

Young men are more likely than young women to still be at home. "More young adults are living at home with their parents, more are living alone or sharing their home with a roommate or other nonrelative, more are living in the homes of others, and fewer are maintaining families of their own. The most striking of these changes has been the declining number of persons maintaining families of their own," notes Arlene F. Saluter of the Census Bureau, in her report *Marital Status and Living Arrangements: March 1990.*

90

"In 1990, the large majority of young adults who lived with their parents had never married (97 percent of 18-to-24-year-olds and 80 percent of 25-to-34-year-olds); the proportion who lived with their parents and who had children of their own present was 4 percent and 13 percent, respectively."

YOUNG ADULTS LIVING AT HOME

Year	18-to-24-year-olds in the parental nest
1960	43%
1970	47
1980	48
1990	53
1992	53

source: U.S. Bureau of the Census

News accounts and other anecdotal evidence suggest that 1990–91 cloudy job prospects propelled some busters back home with the folks. Exorbitant rents through much of the 1980s and even in the soft real-estate market of the early 1990s convinced many busters they could find better digs, more friendly landlords, and significantly lower rent at home. Instead of dropping several hundred dollars a month in rent they'll never see again, stay-at-home busters are smartly building up their nest eggs for the time when they are ready to buy their own place.

Perhaps the biggest factor behind the stay-at-home boom is rising age at first marriage. Young Americans are increasingly postponing marriage to complete their education and launch their careers. Busters are marrying later than any generation of the 20th century. The median age at first marriage in 1992 was 26.5 for men and 24.4 for women. That's higher than it was in 1890. As recently as 1975, when a lot of baby boomers were getting married, the median age at first marriage was 23.5 for men and 21.1 for women. The lowest median marriage age in this century was reached in 1956—22.5 for men and 20.1 for women. At the same time, the proportion who never marry appears to be rising. It may approach 10 percent for busters, up from the historical average of 5 percent.

91

Reasons frequently cited for postponing marriage are to finish college or graduate school, establish a career, build up the nest egg, sow wild oats, wait for the right someone, worry about repeating the mistakes of divorced parents, or simply a desire not to marry now or any time soon.

Some observers suggest that in waiting longer to marry, couples who eventually do marry are theoretically more mature and more secure financially, which should improve the odds for a successful marriage. And, in fact, divorce rates have been declining slightly in recent years for young adults. Still, while busters may divorce less than boomers, many are still divorcing, which is also contributing to an increase in young adults—typically women—returning to their parents' home, with young children in tow.

No doubt, money or the lack of money is a major factor fueling the live-at-home trend. Census Bureau data show that the income of young people maintaining their own households actually declined during the 1980s by over 10 percent.

RISING AGE AT FIRST MARRIAGE

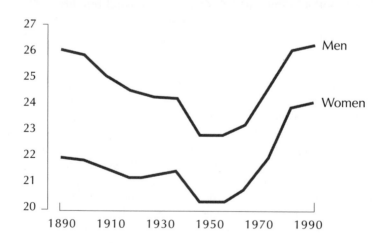

source: U.S. Bureau of the Census

During that same period, all households saw real inflation-adjusted income rise 6.5 percent. Income of middle-aged households, which includes many baby boomers, grew a mere 4 percent. Seniors scored the big gains. Household income of those aged 65 and older grew 20 percent during the 1980s, thanks to generous Social Security and pension benefits.

Busters as well as boomers have been hit by the economy's uneven performance and the late 1980s shakeout in the corporate world. Busters have also been hampered by the skyrocketing costs of college tuition.

"Young adults—people in their 20s—are clearly nowhere as well off today as they were ten years ago," reports Peter Francese, publisher of *American Demographics*. "It has meant lower spending, delayed spending, delayed marriage, all sorts of negative things for consumer markets."

Yes, but what has been obscured in household income figures are busters who are smartly staying longer with their parents. They may be delaying some purchases or investments, such as a home or refrigerator or furnishings. But they are not foregoing them forever. Rather, there is a growing pent-up demand that sooner or later will kick in, giving merchants a tremendous boost in sales when busters feel ready.

Additionally, the ones who are staying home longer, thereby keeping their expenses low, have more discretionary money to spend now on luxury items that they might not otherwise buy if they had the burden of paying exorbitant rents or a mortgage. Thus, the at-home buster is actually a very attractive target for marketers of such luxuries as entertainment, liquor, food, vacation travel, fashion clothes, and cars.

And yes, while average household income of busters now maintaining their own households is less than it was for their age group a decade ago, busters living with their parents are collectively adding many billions of dollars to their families' total household income. That is obscured in government tabulations, which lump income of all household members together and provide no breakouts for individual members. That might cause a marketer or institution to foolishly overlook or dismiss busters at home.

And even though buster household income is comparatively low now, inevitably it will rise. As Peter Francese points out: "Certainly in the 1990s, the best way to get ahead economically is to get a college education. This is so obvious. Households headed by college graduates increased their inflation-adjusted income by 17 percent in the 1980s; even those with some college rose 13 percent."

• VOX BUSTER •

"I like to travel. I like to go to Utah. I like to spend 14 or 15 days on the boards (skiing). I mean I'll go through a couple of thousand dollars out there or more. I enjoy these things. I enjoy wearing nice clothes. I enjoy driving a nice car. And I would not be able to do these things as much (if I was not still living at home)."

Robert Harvey, 28, Short Hills, New Jersey

In flapping back to the parental nest, or staying put longer than did boomers, busters are actually returning to a longstanding pattern. With the exception of baby boomers, an adventurous generation given to flaunting convention, young Americans have typically stayed at home with their parents into their mid-20s, and/or until they marry.

The mass media, in yet another example of simplistic and over-reaching analysis, like to portray the trend of busters' returning/staying home as a clear matter of timidity, abdication of responsibility and freedoms won by boomers, and ultimately an astounding buster defeat. It's no such thing.

Here They Come; There They Go; Here They Come Again

94

Martha Farnsworth Riche of the Population Reference Bureau thinks that staying longer in the parental nest is a logical choice in a risky era when young people are confronted with a dizzying array of complex choices and consequences. Busters are certainly proceeding tenta tively and with a bit of skepticism. And who wouldn't? We are now in the era of AIDS, random street violence, overregulation, a fast-changing economy, and frank reappraisal of past policies and accepted political and social "wisdom."

Staying put just a few years longer is a way of easing into adulthood, sampling what's available, and ultimately making better decisions at a time when stakes are increasingly high.

In a 1990 *American Demographics* article, Riche writes: "Making decisions about marriage, education, and work is hard enough in a world full of choices. Earlier generations of young adults could make decisions in all of these areas at once. Today, this tactic can be paralyzing and unwise, trapping people in unhappy situations. For young adults, boomeranging is a logical way to sample the options."

She continues: "Because people are delaying marriage, they are living with their parents longer. They are delaying marriage because they're going to school. They're going to school because most well-paying jobs now require a college degree. Full-time students are most likely to live with their parents or other relatives ...

"Critics ask when young adults will learn to make commitments. They will learn later," concludes Riche. "When facing so many choices, the best decision may be no decision—at least for a while."

Despite busters' current caution and doubts, economist Richard Easterlin expects their confidence and independence will grow along with their economic prospects. In *Birth and Fortune: The Impact of Numbers on Personal Welfare,* Easterlin writes: "I believe that both young men and young women will benefit from their growing scarcity over the next two decades and that this will encourage a mutually favorable assessment of the future and more willingness to marry and have children."

Maybe I Do And Maybe I Don't

While a record number of young adults are living at home with their parents, more than ever are cohabiting. By 1992, the U.S. had 868,000 unmarried heterosexual couples in which at least one of the pair was under the age of 25, and another 1,351,000 couples with at least one person between the ages of 25 and 34. Altogether, unmarried couples headed by someone under age 35 accounted for 67 percent of all unmarried couples.

Kathryn London, an analyst with the National Center for Health Statistics, speculates that the overall boom in young couples living together could be due to any of several trends: college students sharing expenses without long-term commitments, trial marriages, postponement of the real thing to finish school or launch careers first, or even post-divorce adjustment.

"By the end of the 1980s for the post-boomer generation, it is standard operating procedure. It has become the norm to live together before you marry," notes marketing researcher Bickley Townsend.

"Many post-boomers edge into marriage through cohabitation. About half of today's marriages begin with cohabiting. And some have characterized cohabiting as marriage without the commitment," agrees Condé Nast marketing researcher Isobel Osius. Townsend and Osius made their observations at a 1991 American Demographics panel discussion on "post-boomers."

For the millions of busters who suffered through their own parents' divorces and are now understandably skittish about matrimony, cohabitation is more a sensible testing of the marital waters than the daring adventure it was for so many boomers.

Osius adds: "I think what we're also finding is that it is a solution for the post-boomers to two conflicting needs: being in a relationship and being self-sufficient. For the post-boomers, cohabitation is marriage without the dependence."

Not that busters completely shun dependence and family values. *The American Freshman: Twenty-Five Year Trends, 1966–1990*, a compilation of UCLA's Higher Education Research Institute surveys, finds that: "Following sharp declines in the early 1970s, interest in raising a family has steadily increased to a point that it has recovered much of its earlier popularity (70 percent in 1990 versus 71 percent in 1969). It is also interesting to note that the gap between men and women has been reduced, from about 10 percent in 1969 to less than 2 percent in 1990."

A 1992 study conducted for *Mademoiselle* magazine by The Roper Organization says: "Unlike baby boomers, who frequently mocked marriage and parenthood, twentysomethings long for the romantic notions of a family life they never had. They want a close family, maybe not as large as the Brady Bunch, but as happy. Yet, twentysomethings fear such closeness as much as they want it, which in part explains why they are delaying marriage and parenthood. But they're getting there—gradually."

Buster Biz

Opportunities for Buster Business

- **RENT CONTROL.** You can't beat the rent at home, which is usually zero. Relieved of the burdens of housing costs, homebound busters are often rolling in dough that they're eager to spend—on themselves. Catalog companies and other direct mailers should fine-tune their mailing lists to tap into the vast young-adult-at-home market.

- **THE BEDROOM AS CASTLE.** Mom may furnish the rest of the house, but busters won the battle to furnish their bedrooms. Gone are the ripped wall posters, high school varsity letters, and scratched rock albums, replaced by accoutrements of contemporary young adulthood: CD players, computers, cameras, skis, and the keys to a late-model car parked in the driveway. In the closet is an ever-expanding wardrobe of clothes for every occasion, mood, and season. On the floor are at least a dozen pairs of footwear, with and without spikes. And busters' decorating influence often spreads to other rooms in the house. A buster of our acquaintance finally convinced her mother to change the living-room color scheme from 1960s' harvest gold to peach and moss. Somebody's got to sell them all this stuff.

- **PAPER OR PLASTIC?** They may be living with their folks, but homebound busters are often buying their own groceries, in part because their tastebuds are so different from those of their parents. Markets in buster strongholds should be sure to stock up on dolphin-safe tuna and other buster favorites. And be aware that supermarkets are now prime spots for social encounters. The Safeway at the Watergate complex in Washington, D.C., is nicknamed the "Social Safeway," because of all the singles who patronize it.

- **REAL ESTATE.** Sooner or later, busters are going to fly the parental coop for their own digs. Perhaps not soon enough for their parents, but a flood of busters will eventually turn to realtors, roommate-matching services, and landlords in the search for their own houses.

- **HERE COMES THE BRIDE—SLOWLY BUT SURELY.** While they're sticking close to home now, the vast majority of busters will marry sooner or later. And as surveys show, busters long for romance. Unlike many boomers, busters may be more receptive to traditional weddings with all the trappings before, during, and after the big day.

CHAPTER NINE

A Culture All Their Own

Above and below ground, busters are fashioning their own way of doing, viewing, and saying things. When not mountain climbing or hacking away at their computers, busters are apt to be out at a club for a night of moshing.

Dinner is served: a charcoaled London broil, marinated with a blend of honey, garlic, ginger, green onions, and light soy sauce. The handful of hungry guests sits down at the linen-covered table. Serving plates are passed amid a steady stream of banter and laughter.

Everybody in turn spears the thin, medium-rare strips of steak onto their plates. Then comes the baked potato and romaine lettuce salad with Dijon dressing. A selection of soft drinks and beers is offered. The choice of beers, both environmentally correct, is Coors or Rolling Rock, brewed with all-natural ingredients and pure, crystal-clear mountain water.

The animated conversation ranges from college basketball to the NFL and on to Social Security and funny happenings at previous gatherings. Nobody has qualms about seconds and thirds. After dinner, everyone adjourns to the den to catch some of the pro sports action on the TV. The dial is briefly turned to check out "Murphy Brown." Nobody smokes before or after dinner.

99

This is no power dinner among upwardly mobile suburban neighbors or office colleagues. It's just a boys' night out—1990s style. These are bachelor buster buddies. Most still live at home with their parents.

They get together occasionally, which often winds up being dinner at one of their homes–more precisely their parents' home, usually when the folks are out. It might be a casual barbecue in the backyard or a sit-down dinner; the host usually does the cooking—and with no complaints.

"Pretty much all of my friends are good cooks," says Michael Karl, 28, a banker in suburban New Jersey and tonight's host and chef. "I do see this as the future. I'd say within five years this will be the norm—eating at a table like this for dinner," says pal and dinner guest Jonathan Ukeiley, 28, a bond rating analyst in New York City.

Banker Robert Harvey, also 28, and a guest at dinner that night, admits: "I pride myself on cooking, actually." Adds Ukeiley: "I do, too. Actually, I don't let my girlfriend do any of the cooking."

Harvey recalls that he first learned to cook at Boy Scout summer camp, where each scout had to take a turn preparing dinner for his tentmates. There was no McDonald's in sight. The experience at camp came in handy during the school year, when Harvey occasionally prepared meals for himself and his two younger sisters. "Maybe it's because my mom was working. She was a teacher."

With so many of their mothers holding down jobs, buster boys as well as girls early learned their way around a stove and how to decipher the measuring instructions in recipes. Michael Karl, whose tasty formula for marinated London broil came from his mother's cookbook, reports: "When I served it before, people have called for the recipe."

Fun and Friends, Without Hangovers

There's still a bar scene for busters of drinking age, but it's more cautious in the era of AIDS than in the less-inhibited 1960s and 1970s. Today's watering hole is often a sports bar with a big-screen TV to catch the latest pro or college game.

100

Many busters are opting for a new style of singles socializing—small groups going out for dinner, or to someone's home to eat and catch a game on TV or a movie on the VCR; or regular participation in what sociologists call "affinity groups." These are clubs organized around a shared hobby or interest, or participatory teams, such as the running clubs that can be found in almost every city and metropolitan area.

These days, upwardly mobile singles are as careful about their socializing as they are about their careers. As a result, singles bars may still jump—but so do fitness clubs, libraries, amateur theatrical groups, running clubs, and churches. Churches and clubs give singles a way of meeting people who have more in common than a pitcher of beer. A 1992 Roper Report for *Mademoiselle* magazine finds that women in their 20s are the "night owls of the nineties. Twentysomething women are looking for excitement in their night-lives. They are active and social. And their spare time is their own, to indulge themselves with fun and entertainment." Three-quarters of the young women surveyed said that going to the movies or going to the beach/lake rated as a "good time." Two-thirds cited going dancing. Only 28 percent said that going to a lounge or bar is "a good time."

Swimming, biking, camping, working out, and running are also among the top recreational pursuits of busters, each claiming over 10 million regular buster participants.

Given their environmental and fitness bent, busters are especially drawn to outdoor activities and typically take advantage of natural amenities close by. That might mean skiing during the winter or heading to the Cape on summer weekends in New England, surfing or golfing year-round in southern California, or sailing and swimming anytime in Florida.

"With the guys I hang around with, it's basically football, baseball, and rodeo. And I should have mentioned fishing. A lot of us go fishing all the time," says Jason Palmer, 21, who lives in the Oklahoma town of Weatherford. "My roommate's probably got one of the best ponds in western Oklahoma. We fish for bass."

Palmer, a second-year engineering student at Southwestern Oklahoma University, adds: "I participate in ranch rodeo. It's not really your arena rodeo. You go out and you're timed on things like milking a cow, branding a cow, roping, and how well your horse handles. It's kind of fun."

Then there's the "underground"—not the subway system in London, but the buster music scene in America, which busters would rather the rest of us not know about. For once, something is all their own, and they don't want to lose it. Groups of the underground world include post-punk bands like Nirvana and Helmet, who are starting to get discovered above-ground, to the regret of busters.

Mosh, Mosh the Night Away

Back below ground, when a band turns up the amps and starts screaming and the kids race onto the dance floor, don't expect to see any hustle, watusi, pony, or swim. That was boomer ballroom dancing. The latest buster minuet is slam-dancing, also known as "moshing."

As the music blares, often with words unintelligible to the normal adult ear, pulsating buster bodies run, leap, and collide in mid-air, like human bumper cars. "It's almost like a rugby scrum. There are no rules," says Dan Holland, 24, an occasional slam dancer. "It symbolizes the ultimate urban experience, manifesting this overcrowded, urban feeling. You're right in the middle of pushy, sweaty, gross people."

Moshing injuries, especially bruising, are not unheard of. Buster Holland, a competitive runner who normally tries to avoid leg and foot injuries that could hamper his athletic career, sustained a charley horse recently after being kicked in the calf during a particularly enthusiastic slam dance to the live accompaniment of Helmet, one of his favorite groups. Holland has also had his shirt ripped while moshing. "So generally people go with substandard clothing for that reason," he explains.

While he himself is neat and normally dresses in the preppy style, Holland describes a currently popular fashion statement in the underground as "punk meets hippie, a retro look featuring plaid lumberjack shirt, cutoff shorts, long johns, Doc Marten's or combat boots." The guys affecting the look usually forego shaving for a few days to ensure having a nice stubble on their faces.

"I would argue that maybe we liked it better before, when it was all ours," admits Michael Vazquez, 24, an editor by day who volunteers nights as a deejay on college radio in Cambridge, Massachusetts. "Until Nirvana broke in late '91, punk rock could still be something that had escaped media attention or that most people thought had died in 1978, which it didn't. There have been creative responses by young people, especially in the 1980s. In the early 1980s, there was a thing in American music that I think will be picked up by cultural historians called hardcore, which was a sort of youth movement started by 14- and 15-year-olds."

Curiously, raising the drinking age in the 1980s in many states from 18 to 21 has contributed to the emergence of buster music and the 'underground' culture. "If you were between the ages of 18 and 21 and wanted to go to a club to see bands or to sort of have your own local culture, you couldn't do it because you couldn't get in," says Vasquez, who grew up in suburban Detroit and now lives in Boston.

"This is the crazy amazing thing. They began hanging out in VFW halls, at Unitarian churches, wherever there was a small space available" for bands to play and kids to gather, says Vasquez. "It was a very anti-corporate attitude and a very anti-corporate ethic. The thing about hardcore shows, in an age when ticket prices for large shows were becoming incredibly inflated, like $30 for a lawn ticket, hardcore shows categorically say you get three bands for five bucks."

For example, the Old Cambridge Baptist Church in Boston periodically has underground rock shows put on by entrepreneurial buster bands that draw several hundred teens and twentysomethings, all sipping soft drinks and slam dancing or hip hopping the night away.

"The success that Nirvana had is a really signal thing. Maybe it sort of signals the death knell of my culture or at least the underground status of my culture" worries Vasquez. "Today, the record industry, because they discovered through a fluke that this band had widespread potential, has begun signing tiny little talents all over the place. One of the main things that happens in the underground now is that it's sort of like a weird guessing game as to who's going to get signed next and whether they're going to be any good. Clearly, the people signing these bands don't really understand how anything works."

Some of the other grunge/post-punk practitioners include Pearl Jam, Sonic Youth, and Red Hot Chili Peppers. "They all share this sort of long-haired, youthful, wild and free aesthetic. And they're all making inroads on the mainstream charts," Vazquez notes. "All those bands are both very successful in the alternative markets and are getting mainstream success. It's an interesting process to see. And it's very crazy and it's very exciting. But it's a little disturbing, because there is this sense of lost control." Vazquez has rock ambitions of his own: to go to Czechoslovakia and start that nation's first underground radio station.

Music is a strong unifying force among busters that often cuts across racial and ethnic lines. "Now when you say rap music, you just can't say African Americans, you've got to say Vanilla Ice. This is a time when you're looking at r&b, rhythm and blues, where you might have only thought of Luther Vandross, now you're thinking of white artists like Michael Bolton. This is a time when white artists and Spanish artists—Gloria Estefan—are on the scene just as strong as blacks and are getting the positive response from the African-American crowds as the others are," contends buster Leland Brown, 27, a youth counselor who lives in Danbury, Connecticut.

He says of rap: "It's growing, it's growing. It's hit the r&b scene now. And I think that a lot of the baby boomers really need to accept it because it's here and it's going to stay."

Asked about slam dancing, Brown admits: "I've heard of slam dancing. But if you talk to any African Americans, they'll say that that's white-boy dancing. We don't get into that. We're not into hurting ourselves on the dance floor."

Dances popular with black busters, he says, include the electric slide, also known as the electric boogie, a dance done by a group in unison. And then there's hip hop, an energetic dance style that almost looks choreographed, with the intricate steps and moves of two people precisely coordinated.

"The club scene is really the big thing right now," reports Brown. "It's a big dance floor. They have a little bar in there, but most everybody is on the dance floor. Every once in a while, you'll have a famous artist come there and perform. The deejay is the primary source of entertainment." Regulars, a racial mix, hit the clubs Friday and Saturday nights almost every week.

Many of today's hot rappers are themselves busters or young boomers: Young MC, Run DMC, Hammer, Queen Latifah, Beastie Boys, Public Enemy, Vanilla Ice, L.L. Cool J, and Boyz II Men.

104 | *Rattles and Games: Busters Won't Grow Up*

"The Goo-Goo Crew: These Kids Suck on Pacifiers and Dance With Dolls. Regression Is The Latest Rage" ran the headline over a piece in the Style section of *The Washington Post* late last year. A *Post* reporter infiltrated area dance clubs, where she spotted curious specimens of young adulthood with teething rings, lollipops, baby bottles, dolls, oversized tubes of toothpaste, yo-yos, rubber balls, 3-D glasses, and Flintstone lunchboxes.

While it does nothing to enhance the enjoyment of the music or one's dancing abilities, a fad in the buster underground is sucking on pacifiers and baby bottles. The strange sight was formally launched in the buster underground when such heroes as Flavor Fav of Public Enemy, Kurt Cobain of Nirvana, and TLC all sported pacifiers in various rock videos, report the cultural arbiters at *The Post*.

"Young adults everywhere are flaunting the props of childhood," writes Laura Blumenfeld, *Post* staff writer. "Some dub it a meaningless fad, some say playthings complement drug use, and others say toys are the wail of a generation."

Blumenfeld goes on to quote busters and psychologists as saying this is all an escape from harsh realities, a mock-serious attempt to recapture their fleeting youth and the nurturing they found in too-short supply. "Past youth rebellions have engaged the adult world. Sixties hippies cried, 'We will change the world.' Seventies punk rockers ranted about tearing down society. And eighties youth were keen to knot their yellow ties and accumulate the financial goodies of adulthood," writes Blumenfeld. "But for some of today's adolescents, there's little appeal in challenging adults, destroying adults or becoming adults. The mess has become too daunting."

These regressing busters are providing a new, unexpected market for toy stores and maternity shops, who haven't quite figured out how to advertise to these second-time-around consumers.

There's no such dilemma among marketers of computers and computer games—just give the busters the newest, best, and most challenging there is.

A certain type of buster, specifically the "computer gherkins" among them, are still hacking away at their computers, playing games, and solving problems as young adults. They socialize through computer clubs. Instead of the bridge or poker games their parents or grandparents played with friends, "gherkins" gather to play complicated, fast-action video games on their computers, or act out fantasy role-playing games. Or they can play and communicate by computer modem hooked up to the telephone line.

105

"Over the last 20 years, video games have been an enormous part of a child's upbringing in America," contends author and computer expert Erick Wujcik. "When you talk about this generation, you've also got to talk games."

In the early 1970s, Nolan Bushnell and his fledgling company, Atari, invented a simple video game for kids called "Pong," and the race was on. Within a few years, video games added up to a multi-billion-dollar industry. But kids eventually become adults. The video game industry began producing intricate adventure/fantasy games for adults as well. These games seldom unfold the same way twice, because of many quick decisions players must make. Their choices alter the direction of the game's adventure, whether it is outer space in the 21st century or battling terrorists on Earth in the 1990s. And pioneering role-playing games like "Dungeons and Dragons" or "Traveler," which appeared in the late 1970s aimed at kids, have been followed by a new generation of fantasy games for young adults.

GENCON, a four-day convention of so-called "gamers," drew 20,000 to Milwaukee in August 1992, most of them busters. "If exposed at an early age, most of the people who get into role-playing games will play their whole lives. You can see it in the marketplace. There are more and more games targeted for adults," notes Wujcik, who has written over 20 fantasy role-playing game books and created 6 games.

One possible byproduct of all the time spent playing video and fantasy games might be sharper analytical skills. "These kids, they attack problems much more systematically and logically than I would think previous generations did," maintains Wujcik. "If you have been raised playing video games, arcade games, computer games, and role-playing games, you are a problem solver, much more so than someone of our generation." He happens to be a baby boomer.

Pals, not Partners

More than previous generations, busters have pals–not just romantic interests—among the opposite sex. Raised under the rules of sexual equality and many of them boarded in sexually integrated dormitories, busters are less concerned with, and inhibited by, the differences between the sexes than even the trail-blazing boomers.

"Probably one of my best friends is a girl. It's easier to talk to somebody that's got a different point of view. I hate to say this, but guys a lot of times kind of 'stereotype.' It's either their way or the highway. It's nice to get a different opinion," says Jason Palmer.

"We just hang out a lot. My girlfriend has a hard time accepting it sometimes. But there's nothing there. We went to school together," adds Palmer of the woman friend he's known since fourth grade.

• VOX BUSTER •

"I think we're much more accepting people. We're beyond all the—not beyond all the protests—but as far as sexual rights and women's rights and that whole thing, I think we're much more accepting. And it's gone beyond. We don't want to talk about it all the time. We just accept it. It's there and that's the way it is. And it doesn't bother us."

—Holly Woung, 24, Washington, D.C.

Buster Tastes: Faves, New and Old

Spin magazine, a rock-and-lifestyle magazine with a circulation of 325,000 aimed at 18-to-34-year-olds, offers a mirror to busters and younger boomers. Founded in 1985 by Bob Guccione, Jr., *Spin* explores the cutting edge of buster culture the way *Rolling Stone* has done with baby boomers for 25 years now.

A recent issue of *Spin* carried ads for such essential items as Rollerblades, Nike sports gear, Fila athletic shoes in neon colors, Visa and MasterCard credit cards, General Motors' fuel-efficient and low-priced Geo, the Armed Forces, Honda and Suzuki motorcycles, "real blank drivers licenses—originals, not cheap fake I.D.," condoms by mail, as well as several brands of rum, bourbon, tequila, and beer.

107

There were loads of ads for albums and CDs by rock groups like Miracle Legion, Agnostic Front, Band of Susans, One Voice, and All the Young Dudes.

Articles reported on controversial rapper Ice Cube; Iceland's top rock group, the Sugarcubes; the latest monster southern band, Copperhead; Rush, Canada's "prog-rock pariahs;" and Teddy Riley, "inventor of new jack swing." There were loads of record reviews and features on college radio, AIDS, spring break, and PETA (People for the Ethical Treatment of Animals).

The 1992 *Spin* readers' survey found that two-thirds of respondents felt that music was essential to their daily lives. What were busters listening to?

· Best Music Artists: Perry Farrell, 49 percent; R.E.M., 22 percent; Nirvana, 14 percent; Metallica, 8 percent; U2, 7 percent.

· Best Band: R.E.M., 38 percent; Nirvana, 23 percent; Jane's Addiction, 14 percent; Red Hot Chili Peppers, 13 percent; U2, 12 percent.

· Best Male Singer: Michael Stipe, 34 percent; Bono, 19 percent; Perry Farrell, 16 percent; Chris Cornell, 16 percent; Morrissey, 15 percent.

· Best Female Singer: Mariah Carey, 35 percent; Sinead O'Connor, 34 percent; Kate Pierson, 12 percent; Siouxsie Sioux, 11 percent; Madonna, 10 percent.

· Best Rap Group: Public Enemy, 70 percent; A Tribe Called Quest, 13 percent; N.W.A., 9 percent; De La Soul, 9 percent.

· Worst Oldtimers: Michael Jackson, 34 percent; Mick Jagger, 24 percent; Rod Stewart, 20 percent; Phil Collins, 12 percent; Bob Dylan, 10 percent.

Stay tuned. Buster musical tastes are demanding and mighty fickle. The next *Spin* survey hits newsstands like soon, dudes. Check it out.

The singles that landed on *Spin's* "worst old timer list" are mainstays on golden oldies stations targeted at baby boomers, which is, of course, the whole point. Down through history, each new generation tries to distinguish itself from the one preceding it as a way of carving out an identity and asserting its worth and independence. My own father, who was born in 1908 and came of age in the Roaring Twenties, recalls that his father was mystified by the music of George Gershwin and Cole Porter, and expressions like "23-skidoo" and "vo-dee-oh-doe."

My parents were in turn mystified by my own early cultural heroes—Elvis Presley and Fats Domino. "You can't understand the words," my father kept saying, incredulously. A favorite uncle, an accomplished musician who played in swing bands, assured me that rock & roll was not music—or at least wasn't good music. Nevertheless, Elvis Presley was invited to the White House and now appears on postage stamps, while Queen Elizabeth bestowed the Order of the British Empire on the Beatles.

Now a new generation is writing, performing, and listening to new songs that speak to the busters. While they may be rediscovering some of the golden oldies, busters find that a lot of the stuff from the 1960s and 1970s is like Lawrence Welk music.

Eric Hansmann, a baby boomer who runs a record shop two blocks from the campus of West Virginia University, says, "I don't see many buyers of the classic rock that's popular with baby boomers." Instead the busters that come into his store like rap, urban rhythm & blues, grunge, country & western, and industrial dance music. "A lot of these kids realize that I'm older than they are. So when I say that a new album is good, they're like, 'Yeah, how do you know?' It concerns me because my business is based on new rock and roll."

• VOX BUSTER •

"I hate the Beatles. The Stones are old. We're looking for something new."
—Dan Holland, 24, Pittsburgh, Pennsylvania

Yet, while they don't like moldy oldies from just a few decades ago, there is a retro trend among some busters to dial back further for some timeless music—Frank Sinatra.

Old Blue Eyes, in what one fan gently calls the autumn of his career, is a hit all over again—from bobby soxers to busters. "A lot of my friends are into Frank Sinatra. That's a big college fad. I know friends of mine—people think he's hip, and they play his records and CDs," reports Kevin Dunn, a senior at Loyola College in Baltimore (and the author's nephew).

Dunn, who is partial to Pearl Jam, also has his Sinatra moments and has the boxed set of 80 Sinatra standards squeezed between albums by Guns n' Roses and U2. He, his girlfriend, and two other young friends also caught Frank's 1992 appearance at Radio City Music Hall. "It's probably the last chance we may have to see him," says Dunn.

Why do baby busters enjoy the music that sent their grandmothers into swoons a half-century ago? "A lot of hot and hyped new rock groups will be forgotten in six months. Frank Sinatra has stood the test of time and survived the fads. He's a classic. His words, his music speak to all generations," explains Dunn. "And he's a pleasant and thoughtful change of pace from the daily routine and hearing loss of rock & roll." This may be a monster trend about to bud; it does not, however, register on the *Spin* scale.

Busters Rate the Tube

The best 1992 TV shows in the estimation of *Spin* readers were "Northern Exposure," 42 percent; "The Simpsons," 23 percent; "In Living Color," 14 percent; "Saturday Night Live," 14 percent; and "Seinfeld," 8 percent.

The choice of TV shows is revealing and consistent with buster psyche. "Northern Exposure" is a sitcom about the clash of cultures between a young, know-it-all physician from New York and his new-found neighbors and patients in Alaska, where he goes to launch his career and pay off his med school loans. Busters have the choice of identifying with the physician lost in a strange universe or the Alaskans who know how to survive in a cold world.

"The Simpsons," the half-hour animated cartoon, stars spunky, irreverent, but likable Bart Simpson. A wiseguy kid with an attitude and spike haircut, Bart has given busters some of their favorite phrases, including "Don't have a cow," "eat my shorts," and the all-purpose exclamation-cum-greeting, "hey, dude."

What the original "Saturday Night Live" was to boomers entering adulthood in the late 1970s, "In Living Color" has been to busters, with an intriguing difference. Garrett Morris was the lone minority in the SNL cast; the other regulars were all white. The majority of the cast of "In Living Color," starting with writer-director Keenan Ivory Wayans, his brothers, and sister, happen to be black. There are also a couple of whites and one Asian among the regulars. The appeal of "In Living Color," a politically incorrect comedy show, has been as strong with whites as it's been with blacks. The latest incarnation of "Saturday Night Live" might not match the original version, but a new generation of SNL comics are serving up hip and biting social and political humor and commentary from the frontlines.

Baby boomer Jerry Seinfeld manages to capture the busters' sense of irony and befuddlement at the world around them in his weekly half-hour comedy show in which he plays himself—a modern, easygoing guy in a too-modern, not easygoing-enough world.

Interestingly, "The Simpsons," "In Living Color," and several other buster favorites are broadcast by the Fox Network, the upstart fourth network of Rupert Murdoch. Originally dismissed by the three giant networks as a low-budget interloper, Fox has become a serious challenger, successfully targeting a younger audience with wilder, unconventional, occasionally tasteless, and sometimes inspired shows that defy the taboos.

On the matter of style, *Spin* asked readers to identify the "most righteous fashion statement." Almost two-thirds opted for flannel shirts; another one-third chose nudity. As for the "most heinous fashion statement," 84 percent indicted bell-bottoms and another 16 percent slammed the 1970s look in general—both clear digs at their boomer elders.

Still, not everything from bygone days is viewed as bad by busters. Two-thirds view long hair as the "coolest hairstyle," while 31 percent like dreadlocks. The "most ill-advised hairstyles:" bald, 66 percent; and the *Vanilla Ice* look, 34 percent.

—NOT! and "X"

What "groovy" and "outasight" were to youthful boomers, "not!" is to busters. As in: "You're a regular genius–not!" Or "Mom, this plate of meatloaf and microwavable frozen spinach is the most memorable and delicious meal of my entire 22 years—not!" The unusual grammatical usage of the negative adverb derives from *Wayne's World*, a low-budget, high-grossing 1992 movie spoof of cable TV and the world of busters set in suburban Illinois.

Three-quarters of the respondents to *Spin* magazine's 1992 annual Readers Poll picked "not!" as the best catch-phrase. The abrupt adverb captures busters' skepticism, their mildly sarcastic sense of humor, their anti-boomer-establishment feelings, and determination to be heard and taken seriously. The same themes run through the music and TV shows they like, the movies they go to, and the books they read.

Busters' favorite authors range from scary (Stephen King, picked by 65 percent) to 'bio-factoidal' (Douglas Coupland, who wrote the first novel about busters, *Generation X,* and was picked by 9 percent of respondents).

Interestingly, Coupland is neither a buster nor an American. He's a Canadian, a tail-end boomer, with a keen eye for the culture of today's young adults. His novel is subtitled *Tales for an Accelerated Culture.* Published originally in oversized paperback by St. Martin's Press in 1991, *Generation X* is the first major work to take twentysomethings seriously, even if the book is humorous and fictional.

Coupland calls them "Xers." Among the wisdom "Xers" are finding in *Generation X* and chortling over as they nod in recognition, are the following:

- "Sick Building Migration: The tendency of younger workers to leave or avoid jobs in unhealthy office environments or workplaces affected by the Sick Building Syndrome."
- "Recurving: Leaving one job to take another that pays less but places one back on the learning curve."
- "Anti-Sabbatical: A job taken with the sole intention of staying only for a limited period of time (often one year). The intention is usually to raise enough funds to partake in another, more personally meaningful activity such as watercolor sketching in Crete or designing computer-knit sweaters in Hong Kong. Employers are rarely informed of intentions."
- "Platonic Shadow: A nonsexual friendship with a member of the opposite sex."
- "Down-Nesting: The tendency of parents to move to smaller, guest-room-free houses after the children have moved away so as to avoid children aged 20 to 30 who have boomeranged home."

Buster Biz

Opportunities for Buster Business

- **CHOW TIME.** It's a well-kept secret that buster guys not only know how to cook, but enjoy doing it. They represent a sizable untapped audience for marketers of utensils, woks, grills, classes, and buster-attuned cookbooks. Most of their pots and pans are borrowed from mothers, as are the recipes on 3x5 index cards. Publishers will make millions selling the recipes of buster gourmets.

- **ATTENTION ALL SHOPPERS.** While they may slave in front of hot stoves to bring their favorite recipes to life, buster cooks must first put in time behind a shopping cart at the supermarket. Mom may permit homebound buster sons and daughters to use her stove and recipes, but she's not going to shop for junior, who's actually a smart shopper from his years as a latchkey child. Supermarkets might want to beef up their gourmet sections and adjust their promotional pitch to appeal to busters, perhaps even offering occasional cooking lessons for those wanting to improve their culinary skills before the next gathering.

- **GROUP THERAPY.** Singles bars face stiff competition from affinity groups, clubs, and teams organized around common interests: running clubs, skiing clubs, choirs, book clubs, salons of aspiring poets. It's the 1990s' way to meet. Members need the appropriate gear to perform the club activity. Clubs routinely organize vacations, shopping excursions and discounts, and nights on the town. Clubs are logical targets for travel agents, restaurants, malls, and insurance agents.

- **IT'S ONLY A GAME.** Just because they first played video games or role-playing games a decade ago, don't think busters have grown tired of them. Many of them haven't. They have just gotten better at playing and want more challenging games. A night's entertainment is often a group of gamers, as they call themselves, sitting around playing the latest fantasy or video game.

CHAPTER TEN

Buster Veritas

Skeptical more than cynical, socially concious and sometimes self-conscious, baby busters are survivors. They're active, sometimes angry, always direct.

Bruce Elliott and two pals, all twentysomething, were out for a night on the town one spring day in 1987. They wound up at St. Andrew's Hall, a popular Detroit night spot known for its hot music.

"This was sort of the one basic place you could go to not hear Bob Seger sing about being an old man. We wanted 'what's happening, what's hip, what's now,'" recalls Elliott. Instead, the house band started playing 1960s' Rolling Stones in a obvious appeal to the baby boomers in the audience.

"I was ticked off and complained, 'When are the Eighties going to start. When are we going to be free of the past?'" His pals, Gene Dillenburg and John Kenney, felt the same way. A few months later, the three formed the mock serious "National Association for the Advancement of Time."

"It wasn't initially a slam-the-baby-boom sort of thing. But we did want to make them aware of just what was going on, and that your past, your own life, is not anyone else's," explains Elliott. "More important, we wanted to say to our contemporaries, 'Don't buy anybody else's past—live your own life. Don't fall for this retro thing!," A flurry of media attention, including a front-page story in

USA Today and a critical editorial in the *New York Daily News,* triggered an avalanche of mail from busters, offering encouragement and wanting to join.

The informal group known simply as NAFTAT is headquartered in Los Angeles, where Elliott happens to work as a counselor to the handicapped. NAFTAT publishes an infrequent newsletter, *Clockwise;* serves as an information clearinghouse and buster network; and promotes its cause through interviews and lectures.

"We decided, if nothing else, it would be really fun to annoy a lot of old hippies, to smack that smart look off their faces. Then, we found out, one, how deep these passions ran among people our age. Second, in just what dire straits this group was emotionally, culturally, and financially," says Elliott. "The problem is in trying to help or bring about a generational consciousness. The problem is since they don't believe anybody, why should they believe us?"

So what *do* busters believe? To find out what a generation believes, "listen to their songs," says Gerald C. Celente, author of *Trend Tracking.*

"The baby-boom generation had their thing; they were going to make the world a better place. They were full of baloney, too," says Celente, recalling 1960s and 1970s rock & roll. "Then turn on MTV. All these cats are singing about 'having a terrible time. Life sucks. I'm bored.' That's really a lot of their [busters'] message."

Sure enough, some of the tunes and groups popular with busters today are pretty grim. There are also hostile pop performers like rapper Ice-T and Ireland's cranky chanteuse, Sinead O'Connor. But there are many more upbeat or at least less turgid performers popular with busters, like rappers Hammer or Boyz II Men, country and western's Mary Chapin-Carpenter, bouncy Paula Abdul, the thoughtful U2s, and the whimsical Tom Petty and the Heartbreakers.

It must be remembered that boomers had their own depressing favorites, like the mid-1960s hit "Eve of Destruction" by Barry McGuire, and Janice Ian's "At Seventeen." They also pushed frivolous up-tempo songs like "Up, Up and Away" by the Fifth Dimension, and "You Didn't Have to Be So Nice" by the Lovin' Spoonful, to the top of the charts.

So, too, busters. Their musical tastes are broad, indeed. As aging tennis great and boomer Jimmy Connors once put it when asked the difference between him and today's promising young players: "I listen to the Four Tops; they listen to Z Z Top."

Issues and Consumption

Stuart Himmelfarb, vice president of Roper CollegeTrack, has been surveying college students on 100 campuses since 1988. Roper's findings are representative of the 5 million or so full-time college students. "On the one hand, we find that college students are a very spontaneous group. They're on the verge of many new experiences, both as individuals and members of communities, and also as consumers," says Himmelfarb. "On the other hand, they are a group facing rather bleak prospects, very limited options, and, I think, quite an uphill climb, which comes as a surprise to many."

Himmelfarb believes that today's college students are realistic. When CollegeTrack asked students what to them were the three most important issues in 1992, over half listed AIDS, and one in four mentioned drugs and the environment. The other issues in descending order: quality of education, 21 percent; abortion, 21 percent; budget deficit, 20 percent; unemployment, 19 percent; crime, 18 percent; homelessness, 17 percent. When CollegeTrack asked about major problems on campus, 46 percent mentioned alcohol abuse. They also mentioned date rape, 29 percent; anti-gay bias, 27 percent; anti-black bias, 23 percent; violent crime, 22 percent; nonviolent crime, 22 percent; drug abuse, 19 percent; AIDS, 19 percent; inadequate representation of minorities on the faculty, 18 percent; prejudice against other minorities, 18 percent; and academic cheating, 17 percent.

Baby boomers went to college during the era of the so-called "sexual revolution" and "free love." A glib phrase from those bygone days that found its way to bumper stickers advised: "If it feels good, do it." And many did.

While far from abstaining from sex, busters are clearly more cautious and concerned about the real risks it involves. Sixty-two percent of students surveyed by CollegeTrack in 1991 said they were concerned about contracting AIDS. Of those, 72 percent were using condoms, up from 60 percent in 1990. Fifty-four percent were limiting their sexual activity, up from 39 percent the year before. Twenty-two

116

percent voicing concern in the 1991 survey about AIDS were abstaining from sex, compared with 18 percent in the 1990 survey.

THE BIG ISSUES

What the baby-bust generation feels are important issues.

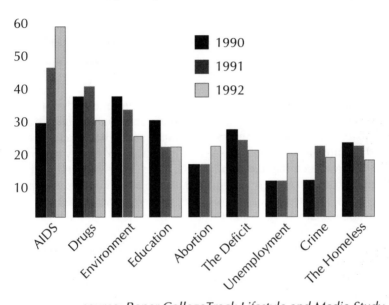

source: Roper CollegeTrack Lifestyle and Media Study
© 1992 The Roper Organization

More than their elders, busters are concerned about the environment and doing something about it. Ninety-one percent of college students are either somewhat or very concerned about the environment. Fifty-four percent recycle bottles and cans, 41 percent recycle newspapers, and 31 percent sort trash.

Half of students surveyed by CollegeTrack say they make brand decisions based on environmental claims on labels or in advertising, compared with 29 percent of all adults. "Students' interest in the environment is in fact translating into some of their personal activities, as well as some of their consumer decisions," says Himmelfarb. "I think it does indicate that the marketers and advertisers who show their involvement in some of these issues can actually reap great benefits in this market."

117

• VOX BUSTER •

"One of the main problems is the environment. It's getting awful ... I think a lot of times we're trying to fix the mistakes that they made—the baby boomers. But I don't think that they were aware that they were making mistakes at the time—like the ozone layer and the environment. I mean nobody recycled back then."

—Megan Rossmann, 18, Centreville, Virginia

Whether from corporate concern for the environment, the bottom line, or both, McDonald's abandoned its Styrofoam packaging in 1990 in favor of paper wrappers. Its restaurants also have racks stuffed with informational bulletins, explaining what the company has done to help protect the environment. Busters have noticed. When CollegeTrack asked an open-ended question about which companies are doing something positive to protect the environment, 23 percent of students named McDonald's.

Interestingly, 58 percent of college students in the previous month ate at McDonald's. "McDonald's having that very positive image in terms of its environmental actions pays off in terms of the high volume," contends Himmelfarb. "We project about 7.5 million visits to McDonald's in the past month by students."

While many older baby boomers during their college years were preoccupied with fulfilling or avoiding their military obligation in the Vietnam War, today's college students are clearly thinking about the economy and their careers. But busters aren't fantasizing about a yuppie renaissance or of reshaping the corporate world in their image as many boomers tried to do. Instead, busters are looking for security.

Career was the most important factor in choosing courses, according to 85 percent of the college seniors surveyed by Roper CollegeTrack. Asked what was very important in their first job, security was at the top of the list, mentioned by 68 percent. Starting salary was not even among the top five. Here's what was: promotions, 67 percent; benefits, 63 percent; long-term income, 58 percent; and creativity, 58 percent.

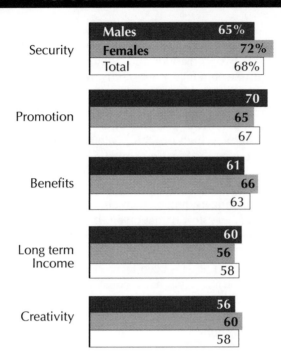

TOP 5 CAREER ISSUES FOR COLLEGE STUDENTS

Security
Males — 65%
Females — 72%
Total — 68%

Promotion
70
65
67

Benefits
61
66
63

Long term Income
60
56
58

Creativity
56
60
58

source: Roper CollegeTrack™ Lifestyle and Media Study
© 1992 The Roper Organization

Holly Woung, 24, a 1992 college graduate from upstate New York, echoes the opinions of her contemporaries. "I am optimistic. I try to be. But it's scary to graduate from college. It smacks you right in the face—the world, especially to come into the situation we're in right now," says Woung, a receptionist with a Washington, D.C., law firm.

"The whole country is depressed. I think people are down about a lot of things: civil unrest, and AIDS, and things like that. And racism that you didn't think was there is there, and homelessness in this city hits you every day. I think we're angry, our generation. These problems are now going to be ours, and we didn't create them."

119

Woung believes that some of today's problems are the aftershocks of the 1980s and the generation directly ahead of hers. "Right now, I think the country's in pretty bad shape. And I think that a lot of baby boomers during the 1980s were paying attention to themselves and being very selfish and that's why we are where we are now," she says. "I think it's going to be laid upon our generation to turn this country around."

For those entering college, UCLA's Higher Education Research Institute survey finds two consistent and contrasting trends. *The American Freshman: Twenty-Five Year Trends,* which summarizes the survey results, notes: "The item showing the strongest upward trend is 'being very well-off financially.' Between 1970 and 1987, the share of college freshmen who endorse this value grew from a low of 39.1 percent to an all-time high of 75.6 percent. Over the same period, the value showing the most precipitous decline in student endorsement was 'developing a meaningful philosophy of life.' Although the latter was the most popular value in 1967, endorsed by 82.9 percent of the entering freshmen, it has been regularly decreasing throughout most of the history of the survey. It continued a steady decline until 1987, when it reached its low point of 39.4 percent. Since 1987, however, the trends have reversed: Interest in developing a meaningful philosophy of life has been increasing gradually, while wanting to be very well-off financially has become slightly less popular. It may be that this recent reversal, coupled with the sharply declining interest in business careers and majors, are early signals of a shift away from a materialistic philosophy."

Its business is rock & roll, but MTV conducted a revealing national opinion survey in 1992, which was representative of registered voters aged 18 to 29—not just those in college. The intriguing and sometimes surprising results, presented as part of the music network's voter drive and issues forum called "Choose or Lose," demonstrate that the young have a lot more on their minds than rock & roll.

The three most important issues cited by respondents were the economy, 84 percent; quality of education, 77 percent; and AIDS, 71 percent. While three-quarters said that the decision on abortion should be between a woman and her doctor and shouldn't involve the government, two-thirds were nevertheless in favor of parental notification for females under age 18 before having an abortion. More of those surveyed believed Clarence Thomas (42 percent) than Anita Hill (32 percent).

Despite the clear turmoil in many of the homes in which busters grew up and the inevitable generation gap, 92 percent chose their mothers as top role models. Fathers finished a close second, at 83 percent. Magic Johnson and Bill Clinton were picked by about half of the respondents; Barbara Bush by 42 percent; and Arnold Schwarzenegger and George Bush by about one-third, just ahead of the fictional TV character Murphy Brown. Parents also proved a major influence on young people's behavior, cited by 69 percent; followed by friends, 64 percent; books, 54 percent; music, 34 percent; TV, 23 percent; and movies, 18 percent.

While other surveys have revealed busters' pessimism, the MTV survey found 61 percent were optimistic about their own future, and just 35 percent were apprehensive. A little over half were apprehensive about the future of the U.S., while 40 percent were optimistic.

The MTV survey found strongest support for the presidential candidacy of Bill Clinton, yet 40 percent of the young people identified themselves as independents, while 31 percent called themselves Democrats, and 29 percent were Republicans.

The survey of 500 young adults was conducted by the Democratic polling firm of Hamilton & Staff, and the Republican polling firm of Charlton Research, Inc. Interestingly, *MTV News* conducted a similar poll of voters aged 18 to 34 in 1988. That poll, conducted in September by the same polling organizations, found Republican candidate George Bush ahead of Democrat Michael Dukakis, 50 percent to 40 percent.

When it actually came time to pull the lever, Bush did get the majority of votes cast in 1988 by people in their teens and 20s, and Clinton was their choice in 1992.

As the 1992 election approached, MTV conducted a second poll that year, surveying 1,000 adults aged 18 to 29. The results were released during a one-hour TV special, "Rock the Vote," broadcast on September 23. The results were a clear harbinger of trouble for President Bush and the shifting political allegiances of busters who had supported him in 1988. By a 10-to-1 margin, young adults said that things in the country were "bad" or "not so good" (63 percent), compared with "excellent" or "good" (6 percent). Three-quarters classified the present situation in America for people their age as a hard time. Fully 87 percent thought that major changes needed to be made in the country.

121

Contrary to the impression of busters as disengaged, 79 percent reported watching TV news, 67 percent read a daily newspaper regularly, 65 percent are very interested in politics, and 55 percent talk about politics with family or friends.

The survey also found that two-thirds of young adults cited lack of jobs or economic opportunity as the biggest obstacle facing their generation, followed by poverty and homelessness (15 percent), the cost of education (15 percent), the abortion issue (15 percent), the environment (14 percent), drugs (14 percent), AIDS (11 percent), crime (10 percent), and health care (10 percent).

"Not since the 1960s has America had a generation of youth with as much to say as today's young adults," commented Geoffrey Garin, president of Peter D. Hart Research Associates, which did the survey. "This survey reveals that young people believe America is in deep trouble and requires significant changes to get it back on track."

Christmas Without Lights

To understand busters or any generation, one must consider the times in which they grew up. "The boomers may have come of age in the quintessential traditional family—that sort of mom and dad, Ozzie and Harriet sort of thing. Then came that loose living in the 1960s and 1970s. The open marriages, the swinging singles—it was a wonderful time to be a young adult, but a horrific and traumatic time to be a child," says Bruce Elliott of the National Association for the Advancement of Time.

"Whereas the boomers were brought up in a sort of optimistic age, with a vision that told you to go out and build a beautiful world and to look forward to the future, by the time we came along there was no futurism. There was no tomorrowland. So, we grew up in a more realistic, really a pessimistic, culture. Watergate took its toll on the American psyche. So did the defeat in Vietnam and something that not really everyone has fully considered, the energy crisis and its impact. It's interesting that a lot of the people that we talked to, the 1973 Christmas without lights is a really big memory. They really do remember long cold winters where it was not cool to consume."

• VOX BUSTER •

Provides a forum for those who feel that interest in the near future is being undermined by a nationwide nostalgia trend ... Believes that "pop culture is so firmly entrenched in the 60s that kids who would otherwise be discovering the world

*around them are wishing they had gone to Woodstock" ...
Marketing aimed at the baby-boom generation has created
classic rock radio and nostalgic television shows that are
"crushing creativity or driving it underground."*

**-entry for the National Association for the Advancement of Time
in the Encyclopedia of Associations**

The tough times that busters experienced growing up are not without
their benefits. "Busters are serious pragmatists, extremely realistic and
blunt to the point of seeming negative," says Elliott. "There is a serious
quest to peel off the veil of illusion and just get down to the real thing.
'What's the real story? Would someone please tell me the truth?' It's
that kind of questioning for raw, tangible reality that I think is the most
defining trait."

In an age of artifice, looming problems, and boomer self-absorption,
Elliott believes that busters could be the irritant and reality check that
brings about needed change. "Eventually, the sibling rivalry (between boomers and busters) will cool down. So, the boomer vision,
this Bill Clinton kind of vision, will marry with the buster pragmatism."

Another trait of busters, according to Elliott, is "fearlessness—a risk-
taking drive from bungee-jumping to strafing Iraq. There's this grownup,
self-raised, 'what the hey, go for it' attitude. 'Just do it.'"

In recent years, a story that has found its way into the lifestyle sections
of newspapers and magazines every six months or so is the one
advising busters that they will be the first generation not to live better
than their parents. The stories, usually written by boomers, are
typically illustrated with photographs of unsmiling busters. Polls often
accompany the stories that show busters to be worried about their
future prospects.

In a 1992 *Washington Post*-ABC News poll of young adults, seven in
ten agreed with the statement that the country's best years were
behind it. Yet, a 1992 survey for *Fortune* magazine of 500 workers in
their 20s found that they fully expect to live as well as their parents did,
and they are optimistic about their careers and financial prospects.
The results of the *Fortune* survey, conducted by the opinion research

123

firm of Clark Martire & Bartolomeo, clearly defy the popular media impressions of busters. The results also underscore the imprecision of pat media stereotypes, the fluidity of opinion, and the strong individual streak of busters.

The *Fortune* survey was reported in a July 13, 1992 cover story titled "The Upbeat Generation." The first word of the story was the exclamation: "Surprise!" No doubt, the results were as much a surprise to *Fortune* as the magazine assumed they'd be to readers, young and old. "Admittedly, their upbeat attitude may stem from the fact that they have already found jobs," the article notes.

The fact of the matter is: boomers—not busters—will be the first generation not to improve their standard of living, because of timing, economics, and demographics. The parents of boomers or those who reached adulthood during the 1940s or 1950s will probably live the best of any generation. Here's why: they worked much of their careers during periods of rapid economic expansion and rapid promotions; they bought their homes for modest prices before inflation; if they sell their homes after retiring, they will realize tremendous profits due to escalating prices since the 1960s; and they will reap the full benefits of Social Security.

Baby boomers will have none of those advantages. Consequently, they will likely be the first generation not to surpass their parents in living standards. Busters will face less competition from one another for jobs and also for housing, although they will bear an unusually heavy load in keeping Social Security afloat.

At least, that's the theory of "generational size." But as we've seen, several factors complicate the prospects for busters: the turmoil and failings of the American educational system, the economy's slowing growth and shift to high-tech and services, and the emergence of a lean and mean corporate structure to do battle in the global marketplace.

These changes, of course, affect workers of all ages. Busters, at least, have the advantage of youth and adaptability. And while poorly educated busters will not have as many high-paying manufacturing jobs to fall back on as previous generations did, well-educated and properly trained busters will definitely be in demand. It remains to be seen just how close, on average, busters can come to achieving the standard of living of today's retirees or even baby boomers. But certainly, many skilled and educated busters have the potential to approach, or even surpass, the living standards of their elders through hard work.

Older people today for the most part amassed what they now have usually through the efforts of a single wage-earner, typically the husband. Inflation, coupled with changes in the economy and society, have meant that many more families now need both husband and wife working to reach and maintain a comfortable level of affluence. Whether they're doing it out of career ambition or necessity, more and more young wives are, indeed, working, which is the way that busters can duplicate the affluence of previous generations. Busters may even be able to surpass boomers in household income, if they are more successful at staying married than the divorce-prone boomers.

The statistics are clear: divorce and female-headed households increase the risk of poverty for women and children. Conversely, marriage provides the opportunity to have two earners contributing to household income, and thus boosts the ability to achieve a high standard of living. What Cheryl Russell wrote in her 1987 book, *100 Predictions for the Baby Boom,* applies to baby busters as well: "The best insurance for affluence is a marriage certificate. And the importance of marriage is growing."

Forget YUPPIES, Now It's YIFFIES

In 1980, *Fortune* magazine took a close look at the hard-charging baby boomers then entering the corporate fast-track. The magazine's writers and editors coined the phrase "yuppies" to describe them: young, upwardly mobile professionals, who viewed business as "the fastest means of gratifying their frankly materialistic requirements."

A decade later, *Fortune* examined busters in the corporate world. "Let's call them yiffies, for young, individualistic, freedom-minded, and few. ... They certainly aren't impassioned about political or social issues. Nobody would describe them as a bunch of activists," advised *Fortune* in a 1990 cover story by Alan Deutschman, based on interviews with over 30 college-educated busters, plus focus groups with other busters and elders.

125

"The busters insist on getting satisfaction from their jobs, but refuse to make personal sacrifices for the sake of the corporation. Their attitude: other interests—leisure, family, lifestyle, the pursuit of experience—are as important as work."

Fortune cautioned bosses: "Sure, you might want to laugh derisively the first time one of your youngest subordinates tells you he intends to work a mere 40-hour week so he can go scuba diving and learn a non-Indo-European tongue. But don't complain, then, when you can't seem to find another competent molecular biologist or quality-control specialist."

Barry Shook, a 28-year-old electrical engineer in Peoria, Illinois, confirms a changing attitude toward work among his contemporaries. "My generation is looking for a challenge, and freedom and flexibility and time to enjoy their free time. That's a lot to ask out of a job. Consequently, I think they're probably more likely to have higher turnover rates of people in our age group. I think they're not afraid to make those changes even in the times that we're in now."

And despite a looming crisis with Social Security and futurists who predict people will work more years, Shook, like so many of his buster contemporaries, is already thinking of retirement. "Just as soon as I think I can afford to," he admits. "If I have to work until I'm 60 or 62, I will. But if there's any way I can work it so I can stop at 55 or sooner, I'll be looking for that opportunity."

As with any generation, busters form their attitudes and behavior in response to their times, their experiences, and also what went before. The trendsetting baby boomers were raised in the comfort of nuclear families. Many of them then proceeded to varying degrees to rebel against their parents, the establishment, and cultural conventions.

Certainly, much good came from the boomers' activism, which greatly contributed to the civil rights movement, affirmative action, women's rights, growing citizen involvement and volunteerism, and ending the Vietman War. But there was also a downside to boomers' trailblazing: drug experimentation and abuse, casual sex that spread disease, schools and educators battered and weakened by too many protests.

126

Boomers promoted and supported many of the reforms and what evolved out of them. Yet, the busters—not the boomers—experienced the full force of those far-reaching changes: working mothers and too-often-absent fathers; fractured and reconfigured families; shifting standards of right and wrong; overly busy schoolhoods spent being chauffeured from one organized activity to another; attending schools and colleges where often puzzling debates rage over what should and shouldn't be taught, while course requirements are being scrapped and new ones added.

In the absence of parents and absolutes and with the growing force of relativism, many busters have grown up without being anchored to a strong set of values, some critics warn. In a hard-hitting study that gained national attention last year, the Joseph & Edna Josephson Institute of Ethics reported: "In response to a continuous barrage of bad examples, a social system which refused to consistently impose negative consequences on bad behavior and unprecedented parental, peer and economic pressures, the operational ethics of many young people are simply an amplified echo of the worst in the adult world. Their misbehavior is more often the product of survival strategies and coping mechanisms than moral deficiency."

Based on a survey of 8,965 young people, the Josephson Institute found that one in three high schoolers and 16 percent of college students admitted to having shoplifted at least once; 61 percent of high schoolers and 32 percent of collegians admitted to having cheated on an exam at least once; over half admitted lying to their parents; and over one-third of college students lied to bosses or customers at work. One-third of high schoolers and college students say they are willing to lie on a resumé, application, or interview to get a job they want.

While believing that behavior among young people has worsened, indeed, the study conceded that there are no similar surveys for previous generations to permit comparisons. "But whether things are measurably worse or not, they are clearly bad enough," asserted the Josephson study.

On the plus side, the study finds that among college students, 58 percent feel an "ethical obligation" to give to charity; 75 percent say making a difference in the lives of others is very important; and 51 percent say doing volunteer work for a worthy cause is important. And, in fact, 68 percent of high schoolers and 73 percent of those in college did charity volunteer work at least once in the previous 12 months. Fully 38 percent of collegians did such work at least five times in the previous year.

Good and bad, busters are what their parents and society around them have made them, taught, and told them. Certainly, a major detrimental influence on busters' lives has been television. Used by parents as babysitters and by Hollywood writers as conduits of mindless trash, TV has promoted moral equivocation.

In their provocative 1991 book, *Watching America,* authors S. Robert Lichter, Linda S. Lichter, and Stanley Rothman examine the fallout. The authors quote Herbert London, a New York University dean who has conducted focus groups with teenagers. London reports that "insinuating itself into our conversations was the extent to which nighttime soap-opera characters serve as models to be emulated ... Do the ends justify the means? ... Yes, say students who watch television regularly."

The authors go on to quote social commentator and iconoclastic Hollywood writer Ben Stein observing: "Television makes people want to be business people, but it also tells them that to be a business executive you have to be an unscrupulous creep...The mores you see now [in the insider trading scandals on Wall Street] are the mores of 'Dallas' and 'Dynasty.' It's not just coincidence."

The news media in recent years have reported an apparent resurgence of bigotry on campus, with commentary that suggests that some of today's students—that is, white males—are somehow less committed to civil rights and equality than boomers were. More than any previous generation, however, it is busters who are more likely to have lived, studied, and worked in racially and ethnically integrated and diverse settings. Busters are truly more familiar and comfortable with differences and more likely to have friends outside their racial group than their elders.

"The twentysomething generation represents an important new era of ethnic diversity in America. This group is less homogeneous, more dynamic and culturally rich than the boomer generation," contends Roper's *Mademoiselle* report, "Twentysomething: The New Individual."

128 Census Bureau data confirm that the baby bust is more racially and ethnically diverse than the nation as a whole. In 1993, 31 percent of the baby bust are minorities, compared with 26 percent of the U.S. The baby-bust breakdown: non-Hispanic white, 69 percent; black, 14 percent; Asian, 4 percent; Hispanic, 13 percent; American Indian/Eskimo/Aleut, 1 percent.

In contrast, the overall U.S. breaks out this way: non-Hispanic white, 74 percent; black, 12 percent; Asian, 3 percent; Hispanic, 10 percent; American Indian/Eskimo/Aleut, 1 percent.

Boosting buster diversity is immigration, which historically tends to be highest for people in their 20s and early 30s. Immigration during the 1980s was the second highest this century. And it's expected to be even higher this decade.

"I think we're more tolerant ... My generation grew up in a social climate where it was not socially acceptable to be racist," says Michael Vazquez, 24. "I was surprised to find how that was true not just of college students but even among a fair number of young people I know who work in the dining halls at Harvard, who come from relatively blighted, white suburbs around here. And they have re-markably liberal attitudes by and large. They're more accepting."

Some tensions do exist and are not unexpected in competitive environments, where different people are brought together, new ideas are debated, and views are exchanged. Ugly and unacceptable incidents have occurred on some college campuses. But it is unclear whether there has been a true increase over previous decades or if any upswing reflects better monitoring by authorities, a greater willing-ness than before to report incidents, a broader range of behavior now considered unacceptable, or a combination of the above.

"I think you're always going to have an incidence of racial tension for as long as the earth exists, because it has always been that way, ever since the days of the Bible when the Jews were enslaved by Egyptians, again one race against the other. So, I mean nothing has changed. Just the names and faces have changed," contends Leland Brown, 27, who is African American.

Yet, he also sees progress. "Definitely, we've been more open. We've had our problems, but overall, we've been more open with other races than in the past. And I think one reason that's behind that, is we, our generation, is the aftermath of the civil rights movement."

He's seen the changes in his own life. Having grown up in Newark, New Jersey, in a neighborhood that was overwhelmingly black and Hispanic, as was the public school enrollment, he then went into the Navy for four years where his mates were all races and from all backgrounds. In boot camp, in electronics classes, and on cruises and liberties, the sailors got to know one another and to learn from one another, and became friends. Now a social worker, Brown lives in a modest, integrated neighborhood of Danbury, Connecticut, where people live and let live. His girlfriend happens to be white.

Asked what accounts for the accepting attitude of Danbury residents, Brown responds: "I guess they just grew up around each other." He thinks about it more, adding: "Nothing separates them, except color. I think they understand that. They realize that there is nothing different between them, that you have white people who are struggling just as bad as black people. So they kind of band together."

While certainly there are common traits, as well as issues, among busters of all races and backgrounds, there are also those that are unique to a race. "The most common characteristic among African Americans now for this generation, I think it would have to be respect. I think a lot of us now are looking for the respect as an African American, as opposed to before it was Negro, then it was black, and then it was African American," says Brown. "A lot of us are looking for respect. A lot of us are going back to our roots. This is something that is very common. Now we're trying to do away with black history month and make it a year-round thing. ... It's something that we as African Americans need to be aware of every month of the year."

Brown continues: "Whites know who they are. Pretty much, you know where you came from. But as far as African Americans go, they ask, 'Where are you from?' And they just say, 'Africa.' They know no more and that's it. And to me, you don't really know anything about yourself when that's all you can say. It's important that we learn, myself included, a lot more about ourselves. Once we have an identity, and once we have a foundation, then we feel comfortable about ourselves. ... And we also need to learn about the other cultures, we need to have respect for the other cultures and to understand what they are and why they do things the way they do."

Similarly, among many young Hispanics and Asians, there is a growing acknowledgment and embrace of their cultural roots, encouraged in many schools and colleges in recent years by the multi cultural movement that seeks to promote unity by exploring and accepting diversity. Instead of the old melting pot metaphor, the multi cultural movement speaks of the U.S. as a mosaic.

The Middle-of-the-Road Generation

UCLA's *The American Freshman: Twenty-Five Year Trends* reports: "Striking changes in political identification have occurred in the 'middle-of-the-road' category. From a low of 45 percent in 1970, the percentage of freshmen identifying themselves in this manner rose by almost one-third to 60 percent in 1983, then declined by one-tenth to 55 percent in 1990. While the gains in middle-of-the-road identification between 1973 and 1983 came almost exclusively at the cost of liberal/far-left groups, the decline since 1983 has been matched by virtually equal increases in the liberal/far-left and conservative/far-right groups."

The study goes on to note: "Our data point to a mixed bag of changes in student support for a variety of issues: While more students support 'liberal' positions on environment and health issues, their views have become more conservative on 'law and order' issues."

Busters are more precisely a jumble, or as buster Dan Holland prefers, "a fusion" of political impulses—conservative in some areas, liberal in others, and all points between and beyond. The mix is not the same across the generation, either. While there may be a generational consensus on the environment, economic opportunity, and Operation Desert Storm, a diversity of opinion mirrors the nation's on such tough issues as affirmative action policies, the Middle East, school vouchers, and government spending.

Busters also display a quiet disenchantment and restlessness in the last few years, no doubt fueled in large part by the recession, corporate layoffs, university budget cutbacks, and political wrangling, partisanship and equivocation. In a concerted effort to reach these very same young people in 1992, Democratic presidential candidate Bill Clinton took the unusual step of going on TV's "Arsenio Hall Show," a favorite with busters, where the candidate talked issues and also blew some lukewarm hot licks on his saxophone.

A few weeks later, Clinton took his unorthodox camapign for votes to MTV, where he fielded questions from assembled busters. In addition to a handful of sophomoric questions about early musical influences, favorite band, and astrological sign, busters peppered Clinton with many more thoughtful questions about their job prospects, the environment, drugs, race relations, education, crime, and abortion, among other things. The questions revealed busters' concern for their future and their disillusionment with American leaders and institutions.

Tom Freston, chairman of the MTV Network, told the *Washington Post:* "People under 25 get the feeling they're not really being talked to about their own concerns ... A lot of it is directed to someone else, someone older. Clinton makes a statement just by talking overtly to their age group."

Busters' importance was further demonstrated by George Bush, who followed Clinton's example and appeared on MTV for an interview in the closing days of the 1992 election season.

In a post-election analysis, reporter Anne Gowen wrote in *The Washington Times:* "It marked the first time they [busters] were so openly courted by at least one side of the political spectrum. Hence the Clinton–Gore campaign's constant emphasis on rock songs at their rallies, Mr. Clinton's face appearing on the cover of *Rolling Stone,* and both Mr. Clinton and running mate Albert Gore turning up on MTV.

"Such wooing may have spurred quick rethinking of Mr. Bush's position. 'You've got to draw the line somewhere. And I am not going to be out there kind of being a teeny-bopper at 68. I just can't do it,' and brought on the last-minute chat with Miss Tabitha Soren, who, as star of MTV's 'Choose or Lose' segments, became one of this year's most unlikely media celebrities."

What's Next? Who's First?

But actually, MTV was scooped. Joining the political fray and muscling into the arena of ideas even earlier was *The Next Progressive.* Launched in the summer of 1991, it is the first political and opinion magazine written by baby busters for baby busters. "Our purpose in launching this exciting experiment is twofold. First, we hope to fill a void in today's social discourse. There is no other media forum for articulate and politically active young people. Second, we seek to carve out a new politics, free of the reflexive code words of liberal and conservative dogma," says Eric P. Liu, 25, the founding editor.

While small in circulation so far, with 5,000 readers, its debut is a significant event and may mark the arrival on the political scene and belated acceptance of busters as adults worthy of attention and with a distinctive point of view. Unlike the National Association for the Advancement of Time's mock serious and sporadically published *Clockwise* newsletter, *The Next Progressive* is a serious magazine indeed and is gaining attention. On the left, *The New Republic's* Michael Kinsley, and on the right, *The National Review's* William Buckley, are both subscribers.

Liu and his journal of ideas have gotten curious yet respectful notices from the *Washington Post* and National Public Radio. *The Next Progressive* was also judged one of the ten best new alternative magazines of 1992 by the *Utne Reader.*

Liu sees his generation as the key to the solution of many of today's most pressing problems. "We are a critical generation, the bridge from the 20th to the 21st century politics and culture. We cannot be skipped over. And contrary to popular perception, we will be ready when our time comes."

There are those who still dismiss talk of busters and a buster culture as a strained scrutiny of mostly college-educated, mostly white, mostly suburban kids.

But Liu, a college graduate who lives in Washington, D.C., and is the child of Chinese immigrants, sees much of the buster experience as a unifying force that affects everyone in his generation, regardless of race or background.

"Certainly to an extent, any discussion like this is going to occur more among the college-educated than perhaps other groups in the population. On the other hand, some of the ideas we're talking about, some of the common traits that we propound that people in the generation share, I think, cross lines of class, race, and gender." He goes on to tick off such hot-button buster issues as: Social Security, the environment, escalating education costs, turmoil in our schools, and job prospects. Those are pressing issues that squarely affect all young people—black, Hispanic, Asian, white, male, female, privileged, and not.

133

Liu goes on to cite the challenge of revitalizing impoverished neighborhoods. "It's so much in our shared interest. ... I think young people, better than previous generations, may have realized how interconnected our lives are going to be. How, for example, neglect of urban poverty is going to come back and bite us at some point. That endless putting up of fences and cordoning off of smaller and smaller bits of suburbia isn't going to save our generation. What's going to save our generation is rolling up our sleeves and getting our hands a little dirty and starting to try to fix some of these problems."

And busters are already rolling up their sleeves to fix things that need fixing. The Winter 1993 issue of *The Next Progressive* carries inspiring essays from a dozen busters of all races and circumstances, including one reformed delinquent, who have launched various organizations and programs to address problems, ranging from the budget deficit to substandard housing to job training for the 21st century. It's exciting stuff, and it's all busters.

"There's something out there stirring. There are young people out there who are searching for some kind of definition," Liu argues. "There's a critical mass of people out there in this generation who are interested in things like cleaning up the mess left to us, interested in avoiding the politics of false choices and avoiding rigid ideologies, and getting things done."

As Liu himself provocatively wrote of his generation a few issues ago: "In our neighborhoods and jobs, we live under postmodern progressive assumptions. We have never known legalized systems of racism or sexism. As the children of affirmative action, however, we have grown up with the backlash against 'reverse discrimination.' Ideologically and conceptually flexible, we will think of new ways to provide equal opportunity—perhaps by emphasizing class over race. But while we work for social progress, we will be more careful than our elders were to prevent social civil wars.

"We are, in short, the Generation of Synthesis. We do not pretend—as many boomers did when they were our age—to have all the answers already. But as we navigate the minefields of cultural revolution and counterrevolution, we will pick and choose methods that work, discard ones that can't, learn different tricks of the trade, and fuse together what we need.

134

"As ridiculed and written off as we may be, our generation could end up being the last line of defense against irreversible national decline."

Buster Biz

Opportunities for Buster Business

- **DOLPHIN-SAFE TUNA.** More than lip-service, busters practice what they preach when it comes to environmentalism and recycling. And what others do or don't do for the environment can influence their consumer decisions. Star-Kist and rival Bumble Bee, with their "dolphin-safe" tuna, and McDonald's recycled paper and a beef policy that protects the rain forest score big with hungry, environmentally aware busters. The right environmental policy, plus a good product, improve the chances of attracting buster consumers.

- **BACK TO THE PRESENT.** Anti-nostalgia has arrived, and not a moment too soon. It's a feeling; it's an attitude; and now it's a movement, thanks to the National Association for the Advancement of Time. Want to reach busters? Don't talk 1960s ancient history; talk about what matters—the present and the future, sure ways to capture their attention.

- **ANY VOLUNTEERS?** While they're not prepared to storm the barricades en masse like so many noisy boomers did, busters do want to get involved and make a difference on an individual level. In an era of cutbacks and strained resources, busters who have the time as well as the inclination represent a tremendous potential source of volunteers.

- **GET SET, GO.** Young, mostly mortgage-free and daring, busters want action, even as they crave security in their careers and relationships. They're the ones who go bungee-jumping and hang-gliding, not the middle-aged boomers. Busters, who seek out the excitement they often find missing in their day-to-day lives, are prime targets for the "experience industry:" adventure travel, competitive sports, and so on.

- **SHOW ME.** Although busters are especially dubious of advice or evidence coming from boomers, they are hungry to learn. They are also more likely to trust their own kind—fellow busters—whether they are newscasters or financial advisors or politicians, who "talk the talk and walk the walk."

135

· **POLITICS AS UNUSUAL.** The buster vote does count, as Bill Clinton ably demonstrated. But, they're a fickle bloc, demanding results. Like any other group, they need to be courted on their terms. Given that voter turnout rises with age, more busters will be going to the polls in 1994 and 1996, making them a prime target and a prize piece in any coalition for politicians who can deliver the goods.

· **A SOAPBOX OF THEIR OWN.** Walter Lippman, William Buckley, Emmett Tyrell, and Jann Wenner were all in their 20s long, long ago when they founded, in order: the *New Republic,* the *National Review, The American Spectator,* and *Rolling Stone.* To that list of thinkers and visionaries mounting a soapbox, add Eric Liu, 25, founding editor of *The Next Progressive,* a political magazine for today's young people. With 44 million busters on the scene, that's a fertile field to plow. There are sure to be more journals and other media of the busters, by the busters, for the busters, offering new outlets for advertisers as well as thinkers.

CHAPTER ELEVEN

A Place Called Home

Here and there across America, baby-buster boom towns are emerging, where their numbers are not small and their influence is large indeed.

What baby bust? Where? There's no shortage of young adults in Des Moines, Austin, Ann Arbor, Charlottesville, Princeton, Boulder, Sacramento, or Eugene.

Or for that matter, in Riley County, Kansas; Onslow County, North Carolina; Liberty County, Georgia; San Diego, California; and in numerous other areas across the U.S. Overall, the baby bust hasn't meant a shortage of teens and young adults in Alaska, Utah, Florida, or much of California.

Here's why: Remember this buster truth—the baby bust is not uniform. In some struggling areas, particularly industrial centers like the metro areas of Detroit, Pittsburgh, and Cleveland, the bust has been exacerbated by an exodus of young people seeking opportunities elsewhere. In these places, the baby bust is extreme—a buster dearth.

The flip side is that some metro areas, even some states, have experienced a buster boom, due to an influx of young families and singles. Typically, these destinations are in the Sunbelt states that have experienced rapid population growth in the last few decades. California, Texas, Florida, Arizona, Nevada, and Georgia accounted for two-thirds of national population growth in the 1980s and will

137

likely account for a similar share in the 1990s. Other states with above-average growth—and the job opportunities that fuel it—include New Hampshire, the Carolinas, Virginia, Colorado, Utah, Oregon, and Washington.

People in their 20s are historically in the most mobile phase of their lives. It is a time of many transitions that trigger moves: going to college, graduating from college, joining the military, getting a job, and getting married. During the 1980s and early 1990s, about 18 percent of the population moved in a given year. In contrast, roughly one-third of Americans in their 20s moved in any given year, according to the Census Bureau's Current Population Survey.

Regardless of age, most people move locally. But people in their 20s are more likely than others to move to another state. About 20 percent of busters on the move are heading to a new state.

In an average day, 1,600 people flock to Florida and 700 leave, for a net gain of 900 people. Contrary to the Sunshine State's image as a geriatric paradise, two-thirds of those newcomers are of working age—and many are young adults. During the 1980s, Florida was one of just eight states to experience a rise in the proportion of its population aged 18 to 24. In the Florida metro areas of Jacksonville and Orlando, the share of residents aged 18 to 24 is slightly higher than the national average of 11 percent, and that of metro Miami is close to the U.S. average at 10 percent. These two metro areas rank among the top 50 with the largest proportion of young adults.

The steady influx of retirees to Florida boosts demand for goods and services, creating job opportunities in construction, restaurants, gas stations, hotels, hospitals, nursing homes, and shops of all kinds, as well as in the accounting, legal, and medical professions. That attracts job-seekers, particularly mobile young people. Their arrival further stimulates the economy, creating more jobs.

There is an occasional clash of cultures between Florida's retirees and younger people, especially in rush-hour traffic or when proposed school bond issues come up for a vote. While younger adults tend to support such bond issues because they or their children are still going through school, seniors often vote "no," arguing that they've already paid to educate their children. But as one Florida retiree says, "If it wasn't for snowbirds, Florida's economy would still depend on picking oranges."

The Florida experience is being repeated in Arizona, Nevada, and California; and immigration is adding to the buster boom, too. Net immigration to the U.S. during the 1980s reached nearly 7 million, a figure topped only by the immigration during the first decade of this century. Immigration accounted for 31 percent of U.S. population growth during the 1980s. Add to that illegal immigration, estimated to average between 100,000 and 300,000 annually. Many of the newcomers, legal and illegal, are in their 20s, which means that America's baby-bust generation is still growing and may add a million more over the next decade or so. The Mexican border region has a strong buster presence, due to Mexican immigration as well as the typically large size of Hispanic families.

The Places to Be

Even in states that have severe population losses, certain towns and metro areas remain strongholds of young adults: collegetowns, military bases, and state capitals.

• VOX BUSTER •

People say to me all the time, 'What do you want to do in three years,' or 'What do you want to do in five years?' That was one of the questions in my interview. I was very well prepared to say, 'Oh, I want to be in this office working on this, this, and this.' Truthfully, I don't know what I want to do in five years. I don't think that far ahead. To me, it's more like one day at a time.

—Tracy Birkhahn, 23, Washington, D.C.

In the rural town of Harrisonburg, Virginia, tucked in the Shenandoah Mountains, fully 37 percent of the population is aged 18 to 24—the highest proportion of any county in the country, according to the 1990 census. Four colleges in the area boost the youth population: Eastern Mennonite College and Seminary, James Madison University, Bridgewater College, and a local community college.

139

The young have had a dramatic impact on the local real estate market. In fact, Harrisonburg experienced a condo boom in the late 1980s.

James Madison, with an enrollment of 11,000 students, has on-campus housing for only 4,000. "One thing we see happening is mom and dad come down and buy a condo or a townhouse. And they sublet it to their son or daughter, who finds three or four roommates," explains Roger Baker, Harrisonburg's acting city manager. "They sublet or rent, get enough to pay the monthly mortgage and insurance, and maybe pick up a couple of bucks. Then when the student graduates, in a lot of instances, the parents turn around and sell it. In some cases, we've had people who really like it here. So, if they can find employment, they just continue to live here."

The students and other young people who stay on are a powerful engine driving the local economy—from the several nightspots to the bookshops, clothing stores, and restaurants. Among the more popular bistros is Luigi's, a pizzeria owned by a former student and especially popular with cutting-edge busters. "They have what I consider weird pizza—fruit pizza, whatever kind of pizza you can imagine, whatever you want on it—not your normal cheese, pepperoni, and sauce. Their pizzas are more innovative," Baker reports.

"We just offer a wide selection of toppings, a lot of vegetarian stuff: broccoli, cauliflower, ricotta cheese, pineapple, spinach, feta cheese, white or wheat crust," explains owner Tim Fratarcangelo, 35, who went to college in Harrisonburg and stayed. "Luigi's is basically a cool place, friendly atmosphere, small, a hole in the wall. ... I think we have broad appeal: country types, mom and pop, college kids, and blue-collars. I try not to focus exclusively on one group. But I do consider the young group worth targeting."

To reach busters, Fratarcangelo runs cartoon ads in the alternative college newspaper, featuring Pizzahead. "He's a super hero from Luigi's. It's kind of off the wall, like Zippy. So it's kind of counter-culture, wacko. That particular form of advertising is geared to the younger crowd." To reach families, Luigi's distributes discount coupons through direct mail and the community newspaper.

The clock and day of the week determine the crowd at Luigi's and the music that's being played on the CD player. "On Friday, when it's packed with kids, you hear hard-driving rock & roll. On Sundays, with families, it's more likely to be jazz or Frank Sinatra or something like that," Fratarcangelo explains. "As far as the economy, there are a lot of kids, and they do pump a lot of money in. But they are very cost conscious. I think everybody is cost conscious today."

Busters also influence the local culture, he adds. "I'd say the culture tends more toward the immediate, and not a lot of gentrified culture." He also finds busters more conservative and career conscious than college students during his time. "I think kids today realize it's not just four years and a good job. They know now they've got to study, get good grades, build up a resumé. It's not a given fact that they'll get a good job after graduating ... When I was in school, I'd go out almost every night of the week. Now they say, 'Hey, we're in school; we're here to study.'"

More than 30 percent of the residents of Whitman County, Washington; Riley County, Kansas; Brazos County, Texas; and Montgomery County, Virginia, are busters in their late teens or early 20s. Other counties where at least one in four residents fall into that age group are Onslow, North Carolina; Monroe, Indiana; Athens, Ohio; Clarke and Liberty, Georgia; Story, Iowa; Oktibbeha, Mississippi; Jackson, Illinois; Centre, Pennsylvania; Douglas, Kansas; and Lincoln, Louisiana. Most of these are not exactly garden spots. But most have lively collegetowns, where students drive the local economy and set the cultural and political agenda.

A few are military bases: Fort Riley in Riley, Kansas; Camp Lejeune in Onslow, North Carolina; and Fort Stewart in Liberty, Georgia. "Soldiers are a much smaller target than America's 8.3 million college students aged 18 to 24, but they are an attractive market nonetheless," *American Demographics* reported in its February 1992 issue. "A young soldier's discretionary income can be high, and soldiers often dominate a region. Some 1.9 million U.S. military troops are assigned to 470 U.S. military bases. The average age is 20.5. One in four is a minority, a higher proportion than among college students."

Riley County, home to the University of Kansas at Manhattan as well as Fort Riley, is an especially good laboratory for comparing the attitudes, behavior, and tastes of college students and young soldiers.

Merchants in Riley, happy to have such a large captive audience of enthusiastic consumers, face the challenge of catering to two similar but distinct groups. "The college students live frugally, but what they have is pretty disposable," Randy Martin, head of the local Chamber of Commerce, told *American Demographics*. "They're here for short periods, and they are not particularly concerned if they leave the area with much money or not. A lot of their needs are taken care of.

"At the fort, people have some of the same opportunities—single, living in barracks, with mess hall privileges—but they have their income. Soldiers have more awareness of the value of money." While students may get $20 to $30 a week from their parents, raw military recruits earn a minimum of $699 a month, plus living expenses. And military pay rises quickly with rank, with substantial bonuses for re-enlisting.

Ed Klimek, general manager of radio station KQLA-FM in Manhattan, Kansas, told *American Demographics:* "The general consensus on college students in this market is that they're here to purchase smaller-ticket items than the soldiers. They're not here to buy autos, furniture, or appliances. They purchase clothes, food, and personal essentials."

With cutbacks in U.S. military troop strength and the scheduled closing of dozens of military bases in the 1990s, the surviving bases and surrounding towns become even bigger barracks and cultural bellwethers for busters. They also remain fertile ground for business opportunity. For example, 6,700 Marines and 2,300 civilians are assigned to the famed Quantico Marine Base in Quantico, Virginia, an hour south of Washington, D.C. The troops and their families spend some $76 million off-base each year in the nearby towns.

Businesses that tend to thrive around military bases include insurance agencies, car dealerships, car- and truck-rental agencies, motorcycle shops, used-car lots, auto mechanics, clothing stores, fitness centers, barbershops specializing in the high-and-tight cut, music stores, video game parlors, fast-food restaurants, gun and hunting shops, shooting ranges, and long-term storage facilities.

Up Close and on Campus

Among metro areas, College Station, Texas, home of the University of Texas, has the nation's highest proportion of adults between the ages of 18 and 24. Fully one-third of the population falls into that age group, higher than during the baby-boom 1960s.

Metros where one-quarter of the residents are between 18 and 24 include (in descending order) Bloomington, Indiana; State College, Pennsylvania; Lawrence, Kansas; Jacksonville, North Carolina; Lafayette, Indiana; Iowa City, Iowa; Champaign, Illinois; Columbia, Missouri; Bloomington, Illinois; Gainesville, Florida; Athens, Georgia; Ann Arbor, Michigan; Grand Forks, North Dakota; and Muncie, Indiana. As with counties, most of these metro areas are home to major colleges.

TOP BUSTER COUNTIES

rank (by share)	county	population 18 to 24	percent of population 18 to 24
1	Harrisonburg, VA	11,411	37.2%
2	Whitman, WA	13,374	34.5
3	Riley, KS	22,261	33.2
4	Brazos, TX	38,953	32.0
5	Montgomery, VA	22,913	31.0
6	Watauga, NC	10,776	29.2
7	Monroe, IN	31,624	29.0
8	Athens, OH	17,269	29.0
9	Clarke, GA	25,326	28.9
10	Story, IA	21,344	28.7
11	Oktibbeha, MS	11,002	28.7
12	Isabella, MI	15,616	28.6
13	McDonough, IL	10,029	28.5
14	Jackson, IL	17,275	28.3
15	Centre, PA	34,892	28.2
16	Douglas, KS	22,910	28.0
17	Lincoln, LA	11,596	27.8
18	Onslow, NC	41,049	27.4
19	Mecosta, MI	10,184	27.3
20	Tompkins, NY	25,110	26.7
21	Lee, AL	22,694	26.0
22	Tippecanoe, IN	33,957	26.0
23	Bulloch, GA	11,076	25.7
24	Payne, OK	15,625	25.4
25	DeKalb, IL	19,649	25.2
	U.S		10.8

source: 1990 census, American Demographics

The proportion of young adults in the metropolitan area of Austin, Texas, is 1.5 times the national average, reflecting the fact that Austin is both a collegetown and state capital. "Austin is the baby-bust capital of the world," contends Dan Holland, himself a baby buster who lived there for three months last year. "I've never seen more backwards baseball caps and oversized clothing in my life. It's incredible." He adds: "I was interested in seeing more people my age, because a lot of the northeastern cities have very old populations. Not that that's bad, but

143

I just wanted to see different perspectives. I was hoping that it would expand my education and outlook on things."

TOP BUSTER METROS

rank (by share)	metropolitan area	population 18 to 24	percent of population 18 to 24
1	Bryan-College Station, TX	38,953	32.0%
2	Bloomington, IN	31,624	29.0
3	State College, PA	34,892	28.2
4	Lawrence, KS	22,910	28.0
5	Jacksonville, NC	41,049	27.4
6	Lafayette, IN	33,957	26.0
7	Iowa City, IA	23,867	24.8
8	Champaign-Urbana, IL	39,220	22.7
9	Columbia, MO	24,798	22.1
10	Bloomington, IL	26,740	20.7
11	Gainesville, FL	42,016	20.6
12	Athens, GA	32,074	20.5
13	Ann Arbor, MI	55,435	19.6
14	Grand Forks, ND	13,507	19.1
15	Muncie, IN	22,692	19.0
16	Provo-Orem, UT	49,676	18.8
17	Tallahassee, FL	43,613	18.7
18	Tuscaloosa, AL	26,382	17.5
19	Fayetteville, NC	46,817	17.1
20	Killeen-Temple, TX	43,235	16.9
21	Fargo, ND	25,718	16.8
22	Charlottesville, VA	21,812	16.6
23	Clarksville, TN	28,164	16.6
24	Lubbock, TX	36,547	16.4
25	Lansing, MI	69,927	16.2
	U.S.		10.8

source: 1990 census, American Demographics

Asked why young adults gravitate to state capitals and collegetowns after graduation, he theorizes that "part of the reason is the excitement. Young adults drive Austin's social scene, and, to a large extent, its economy. The city touts itself as 'the live music capital of the world.' There's this district—the other side of the capital, this historic district of smaller late 1800s buildings that have been restored.

There's just one place after the other, packed with live music clubs. A lot of the new music is coming out of Austin," says Holland, himself a fan of jazz and contemporary rock. "Who's going to these places? It's mostly people in their 20s—professionals. And then you have some college kids. There's this whole huge culture of young people. You can see it in their dress, the way they act, the things they do. There are thousands of people who ride bikes or skateboard, rather than taking the car. They're very environmentally conscious."

Holland adds: "It seems like the entire economy is based on students and people in their 20s. These places catering to them are, for the most part, vegetarian places or very small establishments. They all recycle. They're kind of politically correct. There are a lot of second-hand clothing stores. This idea of recycling is really pervasive. It's kind of strange, because it's a double-pronged market. On the one hand, these people are very earthy, down-to-earth, anti-big-business. And they buy all this recycled clothing. On the other hand, they all own $600 bikes."

To know what's on the minds of baby busters, or at least the better-educated among them, head to college yourself. A visit to a college-town today, especially for a baby boomer, is an eye-opening experience, because of the distinct differences between those two generations, as well as the timeless similarities.

The Politics of Threads

The first subtle difference is clothes. Current styles are more complicated and studied. These days there's the popular and politically correct eco look, T-shirts promoting protection of the rain forests and the spotted owl. There are crass commercial shirts festooned with logos of name-brand beers and other mass-market products. Monied elitists, or those aspiring to that status, sport clothes with high-fashion designer labels. Jocks, instead of simply wearing football jerseys and standard-issue sneakers, now typically wear the official gear of their favorite pro or college teams. They also dress according to their favorite sport. Since running is popular with health-conscious busters, the fitter among them often dress as if they're off to the Olympic marathon trials.

145

The "down-home bubba" look and way of life have grown more popular of late and are favored by those collegians who attend lectures and mixers in bib overalls, flannel shirts, and work boots. An on-campus inspection of students ambling to class reveals several other styles to be au courant: the meticulously sloppy anti-fashion of the rebels; the surfer-dude look of oversized jams and Hawaiian shirts; budding poets dressed in black; hip hop; and the timeless button-down uniform of the 1950s Ivy League.

"You're always thinking, 'What do they want,'" says clothing store owner Loreta Lysick. Lysick, who runs a popular shop in the college-town of Morgantown, West Virginia, says her young customers are "like the rest of the population" in that they are highly segmented by political beliefs, socioeconomic status, and regional background. "When I think about my customer, I think of about ten different people." Shopkeeper Lysick explains busters' fashion sense this way: "'My attitude is this.' And you put on the clothes to match it. It's not necessarily what you are, but what you're feeling politically or whatever."

Like an amoeba, whose cells subdivide into many more amoebas, so, too, busters subdivide themselves into what sociologists call "affinity groups," and everybody else thinks of as friends bound together by common interests. The affinity groups discernible among busters are jarheads (athletes); study gherkins (the studious ones who go on to get their PhDs); hoseheads and geeks (nerdy computer hackers who will likely outearn all their contemporaries); tree huggers (environmental types); Bushies (conservative types); p.c.s (politically correct); p.i.p.s (politically incorrect and proud); and heavy metal rockers/punks (rebels who live for rock & roll).

Buster Life in the Big City

There are over 1 million busters in metropolitan Los Angeles, according to the 1990 census, and almost as many in greater New York. The metro areas of Chicago, Philadelphia, and Boston each have about 500,000 young adults aged 18 to 24. They're attracted there by the excitement, as well as the employment, cultural, and entertainment opportunities that our biggest metro areas offer.

146

Buster towns are marked by impermanence, high mobility, and transience, because busters are at that stage in life when mobility is highest. Busters come and go, constantly switching places with one another. This is good news for landlords with apartments to rent, merchants with inexpensive furniture to rent or sell, U-Haul dealers, and operators of temporary storage facilities.

Summer used to be a slow time in towns with large young-adult populations, as students raced home for summer vacation. But college enrollment is at a record high, and busters are taking longer to finish school, factors that have helped to swell summer-time enrollment and boost local economies year-round.

METROS WITH THE MOST YOUNG ADULTS IN 1990

rank	metropolitan area	population 18 to 24	percent of population
1	Los Angeles-Long Beach, CA	1,089,036	12.3%
2	New York, NY	896,632	10.5
3	Chicago, IL	635,629	10.5
4	Philadelphia, PA	505,788	10.4
5	Boston, MA	454,850	12.0
6	Detroit, MI	437,633	10.0
7	Washington, DC	434,619	11.1
8	Houston, TX	352,229	10.7
9	San Diego, CA	336,820	13.5
10	Atlanta, GA	309,077	10.9
11	Anaheim, CA	300,389	12.5
12	Dallas, TX	280,763	11.0
13	Nassau-Suffolk, NY	269,852	10.3
14	Riverside, CA	269,606	10.4
15	Minneapolis, MN	249,935	10.1
16	Baltimore, MD	246,878	10.4
17	St. Louis, MO	233,265	9.5
18	Phoenix, AZ	226,986	10.7
19	Oakland, CA	215,667	10.4
20	Miami, FL	193,876	1.0
21	Pittsburgh, PA	193,658	9.4
22	Norfolk, VA	192,628	13.8
23	Seattle, WA	192,598	9.8
24	Newark, NJ	184,790	10.1
25	Tampa, FL	177,794	8.6
	U.S.		10.8

source: 1990 census, American Demographics

In addition to bona fide students, there is a growing and important segment in collegetowns: former students and others attracted by the youthful population and culture. These people are more apt to be living in housing off campus and to work full-time. They are a little older and have more disposable income than students.

Recent graduates often stick around a year or two because their younger friends are still there, they like the ambiance, and the real world beyond doesn't look so inviting just now. In collegetowns, they're among their own kind, where they don't have to explain or justify their busterness.

Buster Biz

Opportunities for Buster Business

- **CONDOMINIMIZE.** Collegetowns and state capitals offer land-lords opportunities not only to rent apartments to young people, but to go condo. In many collegetowns, parents are opting to buy condos and install their student scholars there for four (or more) years, while the manse appreciates, rather than have them bunk in at dorms or apartments with no monetary return.

- **TWO SONGS FOR A QUARTER.** Janis Joplin, Jim Morrison, Willie Nelson, and Reba McEntire all played in the clubs of Austin, Texas, during their early years. Other collegetowns and state capitals boast countless stars who played in local joints long ago. Cities with young people are magnets and launching pads for budding musical talent and all that it entails.

- **CARNIVORES NEED NOT APPLY.** While the U.S. Department of Agriculture gathers no statistics on the subject, it's a safe assumption that there are probably more vegetarian restaurants, vitamin supplement stores, and recycling centers in collegetowns and state capitals than in other cities or metro areas. Opportunities abound for marketers of sushi and recycled paper.

- **INCUBATOR OF INC.** Rogue capitalists are loose on the streets of collegetowns and state capitals—incubators for tomorrow's corporate success stories. Entrepreneurial ventures range from the nutty to the future Fortune 500. Many of the entrepreneurs are professors, graduate students, and even undergrads putting their classroom theories to work in the real world.

PART III

And That's the Way It's Going to Be

• • •

CHAPTER TWELVE

What Do Busters Want?

Everything! How do they get it? You sell it to them—carefully, and with a smile.

B aby busters are a bigger and more attractive audience for goods and services than they first appear. They and their billions of dollars in discretionary spending are, indeed, worth pursuing.

Sure, their numbers appear small beside the massive boomers. But consider this: boomers are now reluctantly ensconced in middle-age. They're beginning to do the thing that people do in middle-age: save. Their self-indulgent, acquisitive years are behind them. But the busters are entering that phase. And 44 million acquisitive consumers isn't really so puny. If busters were a nation, Busterland would be the 24th biggest country in the world—just ahead of South Korea and bigger than 86 percent of the nations of the world.

They're already one-and-a-half times larger than the entire population of Canada, which is America's largest trading partner. The White House and American business interests think enough of Canadian consumers that the U.S. has hammered out a ground-breaking free-trade agreement to eliminate trade barriers and tariffs. If it makes dollars and sense to go to all that trouble to cater to Canadians, then it makes even more sense for smart marketers to be targeting America's 44 million busters. Not only are they a bigger market, they're here.

151

But busters have their own phrases, images, and experiences, as every generation does. And marketers must realize this to reach them successfully and keep them as satisfied customers.

• VOX BUSTER •

"We're probably the most discerning group of consumers, I think, across the board. I see some of these commercials, some of the promises that they're making in these commercials, and I know for a fact they're misleading. Be as straight-up as you can about your product, without saying that it's a piece of crap. But don't make promises about what you do. Don't give misleading information. Don't give bogus surveys. Don't give bogus testimonies. Just stay as close as you can to the raw facts, from the most reputable people you can get, because that's the only way you're going to build credibility with my generation."

—John McCarrick, 25, Chevy Chase, Maryland

In a take-it-or-leave-it approach, many marketers surprisingly assume that busters will settle for the same products and ad messages as those tailored for the boomers. True, many products and services are ageless and span the generations. But others—vacation travel, entertainment, cars—are segmented to some degree by age. Nevertheless, marketers too often pitch products at busters using baby-boom images and messages. For example, ads for cars and other products have used background music by Jimi Hendrix, the Mamas and the Papas, Phoebe Snow, and other 1960s workhorses. That's great for appealing to boomers. But to many busters, that music only antagonizes.

While not all of the models in advertising should be busters, people and situations that busters can identify with should be used where appropriate. If the product being promoted—such as automobiles—crosses generations, then the advertising should include busters along with boomers and models from other age groups.

One current ad that does this very effectively is for General Motors' Saturn. The engaging ad, titled "My First Car," is the work of Hal Riney & Partners, the same company that did the funny Bartles & Jaymes wine cooler ads in the 1980s.

A middle-aged father and his buster daughter are out looking for a new car for her. Father, wanting to protect his daughter from a high-pressure salesman and believing car shopping is man's work, thinks he's in charge. The independent daughter, appreciative of his concern, lets Dad think what he wants. "I've done this a half a dozen times ... I know how these people operate," says Dad. The daughter thinks to herself: "When Dad announced he was coming along, I didn't stop him. As if I could have. After a few of those places, I was beginning to think he really knew what he was talking about. Scary, huh?"

Then they head to the Saturn dealer. Daughter: "Then I had this idea going in. Dad says, 'Now don't act too interested.' But when I drove the Saturn, that was it. He was supposed to do the talking. But there were no hassles, even over the price. So I bought one. Dad goes, 'Well, it's a good thing you had me along.' The thing about Dad is, he likes to feel useful, and that's cool." Not only did the 60-second ad show the Saturn's attractive, sporty appearance and tout its strong points, but it presented a realistic situation and characters that real customers could identify with.

But John McCarrick, a buster and law student from Chevy Chase, Maryland, thinks that too many other car ads overlook his generation and consequently are missing a big payoff. "I could go down the list of car commercials absolutely not geared to us. And they don't even try. I think they're missing out on what could be a big deal. What they should do is hire all the people from MTV, because they're making the stuff that appeals to us right now," says McCarrick. "If I was at GM right now, I'd fire my advertising agency, and I would go and steal two of the best creatives at MTV. And I would get them to design commercials that we would watch."

As proof of the persuasive power of the MTV approach, with its rapid-fire, bright visual images and the latest in rock music, McCarrick notes: "They got Clinton on. He's pandering to us. And he won. Didn't he?"

One industry in the forefront of targeting busters is fashion. "Clothing companies for the most part do a very good job: Esprit, the Gap, they pick excellent music. Some of their stuff is really good," McCarrick says. "They use current music that young people are actually listening to. You know the groups, you know the songs. And if you don't, you want to know."

153

WHERE U.S. BUSTERS WOULD RANK AS A COUNTRY

rank	nation	1990 population
1	China	1,100,000,000
2	India	852,667,000
3	United States	248,710,000
4	Indonesia	190,136,000
5	Brazil	152,505,000
6	Russia	148,254,000
7	Japan	123,567,000
8	Nigeria	118,819,000
9	Pakistan	114,649,000
10	Bangladesh	113,930,000
11	Mexico	88,010,000
12	Germany	79,123,000
13	Vietnam	66,171,000
14	Philippines	64,404,000
15	Italy	57,664,000
16	United Kingdom	57,366,000
17	Turkey	57,285,000
18	Iran	57,003,000
19	France	56,358,000
20	Thailand	56,002,000
21	Egypt	53,212,000
22	Ethiopia	51,407,000
23	Ukraine	51,711,000
24	*BABY BUSTERS*	*44,000,000*
25	South Korea	42,792,000
26	Burma	41,277,000
27	South Africa	39,539,000
28	Spain	39,269,000
29	Poland	37,777,000
30	Zaire	36,613,000
31	Colombia	33,076,000
32	Argentina	32,291,000
33	Canada	26,538,000
34	Sudan	26,425,000
35	Tanzania	25,971,000
36	Morocco	25,630,000
37	Algeria	25,377,000
38	Kenya	24,342,000
39	Romania	23,273,000
40	Peru	21,906,000
41	North Korea	21,412,000
42	Uzbekistan	20,569,000
43	Taiwan	20,435,000
44	Venezuela	19,698,000
45	Nepal	19,146,000

source: U.S. Bureau of the Census

The athletic-shoe companies, like Nike, Fila, Reebok, and Etonic are also taking aim at busters in many of their ads, through their use of ethnically and racially diverse young models and pro athletes shown in situations that busters can identify with. Copy in these particular ads also appeals to a buster's skepticism, contrariness, self-sufficiency, and budding generational identity.

A Nike ad for its All Condition Gear, which has appeared in *Spin* magazine, shows an adventurous, fit buster in mid-jump as he vaults over a mountain ledge on one hand. The copy reads: "When you're old, and tired, and suspicious, and plagued with doubt, you'll still hear the world calling you. You'll wish with all your heart you'd taken the time to listen to it. And you'll be filled with regret. Or maybe not."

And Burger King is currently scoring with busters in an offbeat campaign that features a fast-talking, wise-cracking young guy, with baseball cap worn backwards, who sits right down with assorted bemused customers young and old, as he expounds on the finer points of Whoppers and other Burger King delicacies. But such ads are the exceptions in the marketplace today.

McCarrick, a Georgetown law student, offers a bit of free counsel to other marketers late to the buster chase: "Don't think we're the continuation of the baby-boom generation. We're not."

Not even tail-end baby boomers, the several million now in their early 30s, are like the rest of the baby boom. In fact, the youngest boomers are actually much closer in attitude, behavior, and experience, as well as age, to baby busters than they are to the first half or even two-thirds of the boomers, who are now in or approaching middle age. This suggests that the baby bust and kindred spirits are much more numerous and have more clout than first assumed, while the baby boom is not really as massive and homogeneous as it appears.

Minority Marketing: The Key to Buster Billions

Marketing analyst Peter Doherty told *Nation's Business* magazine in a July 1992 article that minority consumers "want to see a representation of their people in the [ad] message. When you're trying to send a message to, say, the Cuban consumer in Miami, don't have a generic Hispanic that the Cubans cannot relate to."

As marketers wake up to the potential of the buster market, they're also belatedly discovering the opportunities in marketing to minorities. The two are not unrelated. After decades of ignoring racial and ethnic minorities, marketers big and small are starting to pursue them aggressively.

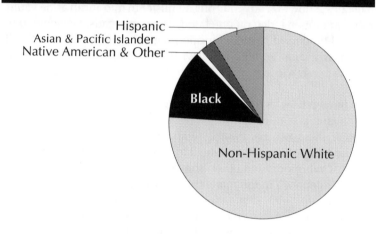

U.S. ETHNIC AND RACIAL DIVERSITY IN 1990

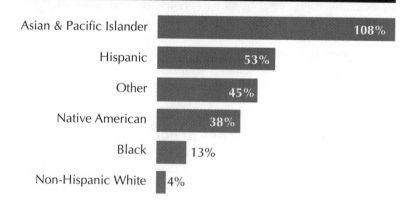

RACE AND ETHNIC GROWTH RATES IN THE 1980s

source: U.S. Bureau of the Census

156

The turnabout was triggered by several factors:

- The national recession and mass markets reaching the saturation point have big companies scrambling for new markets.

- The success of minority entrepreneurs in catering to their own communities has come to the attention of major corporations.

- U.S. population growth is slowing, and with it, sales growth. The 1980s was the second-slowest growing decade on record, second only to the Depression decade of the 1930s. But minorities of all kinds are growing faster than average.

During the 1980s, the U.S. grew 10 percent, while the non-Hispanic white population grew only 4 percent. In contrast, blacks increased 13 percent, to 30 million; Hispanics increased 53 percent, to 22.3 million; and Asians increased 108 percent, to 7.3 million.

Busters are a bigger market than African Americans, or Hispanics, or Asians. In a sense, we can consider busters a minority group. And strategies employed to market to racial and ethnic minorities could be effectively used to reach busters.

Minority marketing basically takes one of three forms, or a combination thereof.

1. It creates a new product to meet the needs or tastes of a particular group. That's what Michael Ghafouri did in 1989 when he launched Kayla Beverly Hills, a cosmetics firm that created makeup and lipsticks specifically for the skintones and texture of Asian-American women. In less than two years, Kayla had annual sales of $8 million.

2. It specializes by stocking a wide array of existing products that appeal to a target group. Pyramid Books, with four stores in the Washington, D.C., area and one in San Diego, carries an impressive selection of magazines and books of interest to African-American professionals and students. When something is not in stock, Pyramid knows where to get it and gets it quickly. Major book chains can't match Pyramid's selection and prompt service.

3. It tailors the ad and sales effort to the target audience. Gulf Atlantic Life Insurance Co., launched in 1991, is the first Hispanic-owned insurance company. Insurance is pretty much insurance. Gulf Atlantic has a strategic advantage in selling policies to Hispanics though, through its Spanish-speaking sales force. It also promotes its policies through ads in Spanish, featuring prominent Hispanics, that run in the Hispanic media.

Chrysler uses various ad agencies to develop different ad spots promoting the same cars to different groups. "The New Yorker ads directed at the general market emphasize safety features, while a black consumer campaign via Lockhart & Pettus, New York, stresses style, and one aimed at Hispanics is aspirational," reported *Advertising Age* in August 1991.

Revlon and several of the other major cosmetics firms market products reformulated for the skintones and textures of African-American, Hispanic, and Asian women. Frito-Lay, the potato chip and snack giant, has introduced Platanitos, aimed at Hispanics, according to *Ad Age*. The snack is made from plantain, a vegetable popular with Hispanics. Gerber Products has expanded its baby-food offerings to include the Tropical line, aimed at Hispanics and made from fruits they enjoy.

Here are variations on the three minority strategies being used to pursue buster bucks:

Strategy 1. Rupert Murdoch's Fox Network, once dismissed as an interloper, is now a serious rival to the Big Three networks, because of cutting-edge shows like "The Simpsons," "Herman's Head," "Beverly Hills 90210," and "Melrose Place." "Fox offers the offbeat, aiming at the teens and twentysomethings," judged the *Washington Post's TV Week* magazine in September 1992. The same article noted: "At ABC, they're back with a pack of shows designed for a younger audience—and for advertisers who like younger audiences."

Strategy 2. A decade ago, MTV was just being launched, with the idea of bringing rock radio to television—a TV network broadcasting the latest music videos, concerts, and interviews, plus hip news, aimed at young adults. By 1992, not only was MTV playing the top rock videos for 35 million teen and twentysomething viewers, they were right in the middle of the presidential campaign, with a voter drive that urged viewers to vote, and news-breaking candidate interviews. MTV has become a powerhouse by featuring and spotlighting the recordings of young rock artists and the styles, issues, and opinions of today's young people—busters. MTV's success masks the simplicity of what it has done: gather together, present, and focus on what's readily available—products (music) by young people that appeal to young people—which most other marketers ignore in their slavish pursuit of boomers.

Strategy 3. Major League Baseball launched its "catch the fever" ad campaign last year, primarily to lure more young males aged 18 to 34 to ballparks and into watching baseball regularly on TV. The series of ads, the work of the New York ad agency Partners & Shevack, with rap background music, shows young ballplayers in action, then cuts away to hip guys enthusiastically explaining points of the game. "Some fan got himself a souvenir," says a buster actor of a home-run with bases loaded. In another ad, a young fan wearing a baseball cap backwards says of a suicide squeeze play: "He's screaming down the chalk." The ad campaign is important to baseball's future, which depends on bringing in new fans to add to, and eventually replace loyal, but aging rooters.

Publish to Busters or Perish Without Them

Clues to marketing and winning busters can be found in newspapers and magazines, which are in a constant battle to retain as much of their existing audience as possible while luring newcomers. The ads as well as the stories found in the media—their content and how they're crafted—provide clear evidence of what is—or isn't—being done to bring busters on board.

To ignore or fail to attract new consumers is to invite decline and possible failure, as existing markets mature and eventually die off or are lured away by competitors. The newspaper industry has learned the hard way.

Total daily circulation has dropped by over 2 million since 1985, to 60.7 million in 1991. Sunday circulation has stabilized around 62 million, reports the trade publication *Editor & Publisher.* The proportion of adults who read newspapers daily has dropped from 78 percent in 1970 to 62 percent in 1991.

While two-thirds of people aged 35 to 44 read papers daily, only half of those aged 18 to 24 do, according to a 1991 Simmons Market

Research Bureau report. Other surveys have shown that only one in five persons under age 35 reads a daily newspaper.

Gannett, the nation's largest newspaper chain, with over 80 daily papers and publisher of the trendsetting *USA Today*, is aggressively pursuing new readers, including busters. "You have to develop the habit and the reliance on a certain form of media now," says Gannett executive Mark Silverman. "You can't come in in 15 years and say, 'Oh, by the way, how would you like to read a newspaper?'"

Silverman is director of a companywide research project, "News 2000," in which each Gannett newspaper aims to rediscover its surrounding community and residents through focus groups, informal discussions, town meetings, surveys, and scrutiny of data from the 1990 census and other sources.

"It's a program that puts readers first. Readers' interests and needs will determine what a newspaper covers, how it covers the news, and, to a great degree, how its staffers do their jobs," announced a Gannett summary. "It's a program that champions the diversity of our communities and reflects that diversity on newspapers' staff and on newspapers' pages."

Busters are an important part of the diversity that Gannett wants to reflect and reach. "If I were in Boston and I was trying to appeal to people 25 and under, I would have some pretty good content on housing and health care, and transportation geared to college students," explains Silverman. "If I were in Great Falls, Montana, I might take a very different approach, and it might deal with job training and social opportunities."

In just 11 years, Gannett's flagship paper, *USA Today*, has achieved the biggest daily readership: some 6 million, a majority of whom are busy baby boomers. While effectively appealing to baby boomers, the paper also makes a concerted effort to reach other age groups, as well as various racial and ethnic groups, through careful story and photo selection.

160 News 2000's Silverman says of busters as marketing targets: "Long-term, they are very important. They may not have the collective buying power of their parents. And right now, they may not wield the collective clout of their parents, but eventually they are going to occupy a lot of the buying dollars in a community."

He continues: "Someday the baby boomers are going to die. And before they die, they are going to enter a phase of their lives where they have less disposable income.

"Even though the scale may be smaller, it will be the bust generation that will be paying college tuition, buying cars, buying second homes, and perhaps engaging in more interesting financing methods in order to do all of this stuff, and perhaps have more two-income homes than one-income homes. Nevertheless, they are going to be the players."

While Gannett's products are newspapers, its creative efforts to expand its readership and revenue base hold lessons for marketers and institutions of all types. If Gannett papers, as well as other media that ultimately are advertising vehicles, are successful in attracting key demographic groups as loyal readers, then the advertisers gain insight into what's important to these groups, what their lives are like, and what their needs and preferences are.

"At the heart of News 2000 is the premise that every community has within it maybe 8 to 12 really key topics. You can break that down further whether you're talking about age or racial groups or lifestyle groups. There are a couple of key topics that appeal to each group in the community. And the first way to attract them is to cover them," explains Silverman.

One topic that cuts across most age groups and is of particular importance to busters as well as those 55 and older is what Silverman calls "survival." Into that category, he lumps personal finances, education, the workplace, and health care.

"That says to me if I were publishing a newspaper in city X, I would look for the survival issues out there. And I would provide practical advice. I would write stories about the problems and stories about successes, to let people draw their own conclusions. And on the editorial page, I would take a stand and become a leader in championing certain things that would give people more of a chance of surviving the economy or the marketplace, or surviving health care, surviving their doctor, their teacher, or their kid's principal," Silverman suggests.

161

"I think that there is a realization on the part of the bust generation that they are not going to be able to necessarily achieve their parents' lifestyle, unless certain things happen. It's going to be much harder for them to do that."

What marketers could deduce from this is that there will be demand for what might be called "survival goods and services" for busters. These might include career counseling, financial planning, especially retirement planning, job training, day care, as well as first-time home mortgages.

While the economy may make it tough for busters to match their parents' level of affluence, their chances greatly improve and might actually surpass their parents if they are married and working in dual-income households.

Whether they do it out of ambition or because they must, working women have increasingly supplemented their husbands' earnings in recent decades and greatly helped to counterbalance the impact of inflation. Bureau of Labor Statistics projections expect rising labor force participation for women past the turn of the century. This will further expand opportunities for marketers, who can provide convenience to time-starved busters, especially working mothers, who will pay others to handle household chores such as housecleaning, cooking meals, grocery shopping, watching the kids, babysitting the house, picking up and returning dry cleaning, delivering gourmet meals, and on and on. The possibilities are nearly limitless.

Ads have even appeared in various city magazines offering to organize dinner parties, pick out personal gifts for spouses and other loved ones, handle personal correspondence, write love poems for that special someone, break off with that no-longer special someone, stand in line, and complain about and get refunds for shoddy service or merchandise.

Isobel Osius, associate research director at Condé Nast publications, sees in the busters, or the post-boomers, as she calls them, "a new kind of reader." As a group, busters have grown up in trying circumstances and learned how to cope and adapt. Consequently, her magazines will have to "be more aware, more timely, and more tightly targeted than we have ever been."

162

New areas for magazines trying to woo the busters, she suggests, might include the so-called new men's movement, with its introspective, New Age sensibilities, and 1990s pragmatism. Speaking at American Demographics' 1991 marketing conference, Osius said, "Where does it leave us as marketers? It leaves us looking at a rapidly moving target.... It also leaves us looking at a group of people who are skeptical and have a lot of experience. Remember that they are self-sufficient, and they have had a lot of life experience. By the time these people reach 15, they're probably about where I was at 25. By the time they reach 25, they're 40-years-old in their heads in terms of the kinds of experiences, the kinds of life decisions and choices that they've already made.... This is a very pragmatic cohort. But I think the flip side of that is that they have a real longing for fantasy and escape."

The old caution of "caveat emptor"—let the buyer beware—might be rewritten for the 1990s as "let the marketer be aware."

Buster Biz

Opportunities for Buster Business

· **ATTENTION SHOPPERS.** The late Sam Walton made billions for himself and Wal-Mart, selling to customers that every other merchant ignored—the downscale. Busters aren't downscale, just ignored by too many marketers. Sooner or later, they'll be discovered by marketers, creating a new generation of Sam Waltons for the 1990s.

· **ACT YOUR AGE.** Marketers obsessed with the baby boom have tended to age with them, only to find themselves locked in brutal competition with all the other marketers in the hunt for boomer consumer dollars. There is less competition in pursuing overlooked busters. Yet the smart marketer must still shift with and target busters wherever they are in their lifecycle. During the 1990s, busters will be mostly in their late teens and 20s and thus concerned with and needing the things that young adults need. In another decade, they will need the things that people in their 30s need and use.

· **MADISON AVENUE.** The medium is still the message. Just as ad agencies and modeling agencies craft messages to particular niches, such as boomers, blacks, or seniors, so too will they increasingly take aim at the busters. Agencies that land the big accounts will be those who understand the buster psyche and use the buster argot, delivering the message to busters from busters.

· **DOCTOR OF BUSTEROLOGY.** Corporations, political parties, and institutions routinely turn to self-appointed experts and consultants to advise them on how to reach various segments and interest groups. For example, there's now a newsletter called the *Boomer Report* that tracks boomers for marketers and others. Look for a new wave of consultants who will figure out busters for a fee.

· **SURVIVALISM.** Unlike the survivalists of the 1980s who took to the hills with shotguns and six months of canned food in preparation for Armageddon, unarmed buster survivalists in the 1990s will turn to magazines, TV, their bankers, and assorted counselors for practical how-to advice for not only surviving but succeeding at home, at work, and at play in an ever more complicated world.

164

· **TOMORROW'S NOSTALGIA TODAY.** Just as today's seniors still spin scratched Frank Sinatra albums on the stereo and boomers listen to golden-oldies stations, so too busters will tune back in time to the music they grew up with. While the 1980s are barely over and the 1990s are still unfolding, the teen artifacts of these times are tomorrow's treasured collectibles. Warning to moms and dads: Do not throw out your children's ZZ Top CDs, Donkey Kong video game, or Batman T-shirts. Store them in the attic. Your grown children will come by to collect them in a few more years.

CHAPTER THIRTEEN

Houses for Sale

*While many busters are still living with the folks,
some pioneers are venturing off on their own to
find digs on the outer fringes of metro areas. When
the rest are ready, they may not have to go so far.
Busters could be in a strong position to buy homes
in the 1990s and beyond.*

Newlyweds Rich and Brigitte Endrulat commute more than four
hours a day from their new Pennsylvania home in the Pocono
Mountains to their jobs in New York City and back—200 miles
roundtrip, five days a week. They leave their house at 5:15 a.m. and
get back a little before 7:00 p.m. "You don't see your house until the
weekends. You don't see it on weekdays, because in the morning it's
dark, and when we come home it's dark," says Brigitte, 26, who works
as a bookkeeper.

Rich, 27, an electrician, plays on a Pocono softball team called the
"5:45ers"—so named because of the bus they all catch from high-
paying jobs in New York City. Despite a lot of talent, the team seldom
wins its games on the weekends because the players never get home
early enough to practice during the week.

Like Rich Endrulat, most of his teammates are young married tradesmen or executives who grew up in New York City or its surrounding
suburbs. They moved to the Poconos to find affordable housing and
get away from urban problems.

The Endrulats, who were originally from Brooklyn, looked at homes
in nearby suburbs. "We wanted to go to Jersey, but Jersey was
expensive ... It's not as cheap as buying over here," says Brigitte. "A

lot of younger couples have come out here, too, because it was the only place they could afford a house." Adds Rich: "We don't want to bring up children in New York City. It's getting too bad. And the country life is nice. It's nice and quiet. You come home to peace and quiet."

They live in a new, three-bedroom colonial on 1.3 hilltop acres. "This home would be worth almost $300,000 in Brooklyn, in Jersey a little less. Here we got this house for $110,000. It's a lot cheaper than it would be there," says Brigitte. Deer graze in their yard; annual property taxes are only $1,000. In suburban New York, New Jersey, or Connecticut, taxes on a similar home and lot would be triple.

While they'd prefer to work locally, the Endrulats have discovered what previous urban refugees have—the Poconos is still largely a resort area and does not offer many high-paying jobs. So they and several hundred others in new frontier communities make the tiring and expensive bus commute back to jobs "in the city." The monthly bus ticket can run $250 to $300, plus gas for the car to get to and from the bus stop. Many also have to ride a subway to the office once they get to Manhattan—another $40 a month.

"Don't think we wanted to move this far away," says Brigitte. "But when we go home, at least we have our own house. It makes it worth it."

While collegetowns, state capitals, and military bases are meccas for singles, many married busters in the expensive areas of the Northeast and much of California are popping up in new, outer-ring suburbs, where land is plentiful and still affordable, but the commutes can be killers.

In California, the community of Moreno Valley in Riverside County saw its population explode by 371 percent between 1980 and 1992, growing from 28,000 to an estimated 132,000. A decade before, it barely existed. Jobs are not luring people to Moreno Valley, because there aren't many. Moreno Valley is practically a brand-new bedroom community in the desert, 60 miles west of downtown Los Angeles, where many local residents work. "Overall, this is where we found the best deal," says Jim McFadden, 28, explaining why he and his wife, Bridget, 27, moved to Moreno Valley last year.

He commutes about 15 miles to work, which takes only about 25 minutes, since he leaves his house at 4:30 a.m. Bridget drives in rush-

167

hour a bit farther and longer to her office in Riverside. The U.S. average—11 miles, 22 minutes to work, each way—is a bit shorter, but the McFaddens are decidedly luckier than several neighbors who travel more than three hours a day to and from work in places like Long Beach, Torrance, Irvine, and Cerritos.

Despite the allure of the California coast, the McFaddens never seriously considered any closer towns. "Reality set in, and we knew we couldn't afford it. We thought about it and didn't even really try, because it would be just too far out of reach. No use getting your hopes up for something you can't get," says Jim.

Not wanting to waste their money on rent, the young couple worked hard and saved, buying a house at the earliest opportunity. Their two-bedroom, two-bath house, which cost $114,900, could easily have cost twice that in Los Angeles or Orange County. "We're pretty tight with money," he admits. For entertainment, the couple enjoys barbecues with their neighbors, visiting relatives, hiking in the nearby mountains, and meetings at the local railroad club, where Jim gets to tinker on vintage steam and diesel locomotives.

Couples determined to get into the California housing market have also fueled growth in outlying spots like Palmdale, 50 miles north of downtown Los Angeles, and the Sonoma Valley, north of San Francisco.

In New Hampshire, an influx of families seeking affordable housing and refuge from Massachusetts taxes helped boost the population of the Granite State by 21 percent in the 1980s, making it the sixth fastest-growing state in the nation. The growth has come mostly along New Hampshire's Route 93 corridor, in historic southern-tier towns like Nashua, Salem, Derry, and Manchester, and along the Atlantic Coast in such places as Portsmouth and Hampton.

In the Washington, D.C., area, which is one of the most expensive metro areas to live in, some people have opted to move to the Panhandle of West Virginia and commute in from Harper's Ferry, Charles Town, and Martinsburg. The train, carrying lobbyists, lawyers, and congressional aides from the affordable, rural beauty of the Harper's Ferry area to Washington's Union Station, within sight of the Capitol, takes $1\frac{1}{2}$ hours.

Buster Home-Buying Prospects Are Improving

Escalating property prices in numerous metro areas on both coasts, plus high interest rates and recent recessions, have combined to drive down homeownership rates during the 1980s. The Census Bureau calculates that the homeownership rate dropped from a peak of 66 percent of households in 1980 to 64 percent in 1991. Ownership rates for people under age 35 declined from 43 percent in 1981 to 38 percent in 1991.

TRENDS IN HOMEOWNERSHIP RATES

age	1973	1976	1980	1983	1987	1991
under 25	23.4%	21%	21.3%	19.3%	16.1%	15.8%
25 to 29	43.6	43.2	43.3	38.2	35.9	32.8
30 to 34	60.2	62.4	61.1	55.7	53.2	51.3
35 to 39	68.5	69.0	70.8	65.8	63.8	62.4
40 to 44	72.9	73.9	74.2	74.2	70.6	69.1
45 to 54	76.1	77.4	77.7	77.1	75.8	75.4
55 to 64	75.7	77.2	79.3	80.5	80.8	80.2
65 to 74	71.3	72.7	75.2	76.9	78.1	79.9
75 & older	67.1	67.2	67.8	71.6	70.7	72.4

Peak homeownership years are highlighted.

source: Joint Center for Housing Studies of Harvard University

Studies from the Joint Center for Housing Studies at Harvard University have also found a precipitous drop in homeownership rates among the young. In 1980, 52 percent of households headed by someone aged 25 to 34 owned their own homes. By 1991, the rate had plunged to 43 percent.

This trend would seem to bode ill for busters who are just beginning to enter the home-buying market. But other trends will work to the busters' advantage. Ultimately, their prospects of owning a home may actually be quite good. As with so many things involving busters, it comes down to their size. Bear in mind that busters are still very young, ranging in age from 17 to 28. And the majority of busters are still home with their parents. But during the 1990s, half of busters will be in their 30s. Historically, homeownership rates jump by about 50 percent between one's late 20s and late 30s. The Harvard study shows that 62 percent of householders aged 35 to 39 in 1991 owned their homes.

"The number of new home-buyers was a prime factor in pushing up the cost of housing in the late 1970s and 1980s. Thirty-two million Americans reached age 30 (a typical age for purchasing a first home) during the 1970s, and another 42 million turned 30 during the 1980s. Spiraling home prices, along with soaring energy costs and the declining value of the U.S. dollar, helped unleash an inflationary spiral," write Leon F. Bouvier and Carol J. De Vita in their 1991 study *The Baby Boom—Entering Midlife,* published by the Population Reference Bureau, of Washington, D.C. Builders gladly cooperated by embarking on a massive home-building boom that converted countless millions of acres of apple orchards and cow pastures to subdivisions.

• VOX BUSTER •

"I think we want it at least as good as what our parents have. I don't know if we're necessarily interested in having it so much better. But everybody wants to have their own home or their place and their own car and have at least what their parents have."

—Cyndy Wrobel, 21, Eastpointe, Michigan

Gerald Celente, in his 1991 book *Trend Tracking,* cautions investors: "As for real estate, you shouldn't expect it to be the winner that it was in the 1980s. The baby boomers, who created an unusually high level of demand for housing, have been absorbed by the market. And there isn't another wave of them coming along. In most areas, the rate of appreciation in the value of single-family houses won't be much more than the rate of inflation."

That's good news, indeed, for busters, once they are ready to go house-hunting. Busters have been staying home with Mom and Dad longer than boomers did—many are not paying rent. They are building up their bank accounts. When it comes time to buy their first house, they will be buying in a real-estate market with an oversupply of starter houses built for baby boomers. It will be a buyer's market. This oversupply will soften, possibly even lower, prices.

"Some economists foresee continued softening of housing prices and an easing of demand as the small baby-bust generation enters the housing market," write Bouvier and De Vita. "Others predict continued high demand as the younger and more numerous portion of the baby-boom generation enters its family formation stages during the 1990s."

Economists N. Gregory Mankiw and David N. Weil are two who expect busters to be in a strong position when they go to buy their homes. "Large demographic changes of the sort we have observed induce large (and mostly predictable) changes in the demand for housing. Second, these fluctuations in demand appear to have substantial impact on the price of housing. Third, recent demographic patterns imply that housing demand will grow more slowly over the next 20 years than at any time since World War II," they observe in "The Baby Boom, the Baby Bust, and the Housing Market." The article appeared in the 1989 edition of *Regional Science and Urban Economics.*

"Between 1970 and 1980, housing prices rose dramatically: depending on the index, the real price of housing rose between 19 and 32 percent.... Our results indicate that this increase in housing prices was largely attributable to the aging of the baby boom," continue Mankiw and Weil.

"Over the next 20 years, the baby-bust generation will be in its house-buying years.... This implies that housing demand will grow more slowly in the future. Our estimates suggest that real housing prices will fall substantially—indeed, real housing prices may well reach levels lower than those experienced at any time in the past 40 years."

• VOX BUSTER •

171

We're like the youngest couple up here. We're starting a new trend."

—Richard Endrulat, 27, Effort, Pennsylvania

"They [busters] will probably be going initially into rental housing. And rents have been declining in real terms over the past couple of years as a result of high vacancy rates. Those high vacancy rates are a combination of, first of all, lower-than-expected household formation rates and overbuilding of multi-family rental housing in the 1980s," notes economist Michael Carliner, of the National Association of Home Builders. "Right now, they're in a relatively favorable position. But the rental market is going to tighten up a lot in the next couple of years."

Despite their theoretical advantage of smallness in the work force, busters generally have lost ground economically during the 1980s, according to various studies. The result, Carliner suggests, may be that busters have a tougher time—and longer time—coming up with the downpayment for the first home.

"However, I think they will have an advantage in this large starter home production in the 1970s and 1980s that is going to give them a relatively favorable situation in terms of buying starter homes," Carliner notes. Busters will also reap the benefits of low mortgage rates.

"I would guess that homeownership rates would rise among these younger groups as well, both because we are probably going to see relatively modest increases in starter-home prices and because we are probably going to see relatively high increases within a couple of years in rents. So, there will be an incentive for them to become homeowners," says Carliner.

Nancy McArdle, research analyst at Harvard's Joint Center for Housing Studies, also expects an increase in homeownership rates among young adults. "Looking toward the future, for the most part, is a fairly good situation for young adults trying to buy a home for a number of reasons," says McArdle. "First, as the economy recovers, which we expect it will, there will be an increase in income for these people. They have now been waiting for quite a while, the ones who have not made it into homeownership. So they will probably have some accumulated monies for a downpayment. And they're a little older now, so they're further along in terms of their income potential."

McArdle adds: "The baby-boom generation is now at the stage where they're more likely to be trading up in terms of housing.... It frees up quite a bit of housing for people who are interested in starter homes.

Now we don't believe that that is exclusively young adults. It could also be people who are recently divorced, older people, people who want smaller homes. There are lots of different markets for that housing. But one of them is certainly young adults who want to become homeowners for the first time."

She concludes: "We expect that in general things will be brighter, significantly brighter for young adults trying to make it into homeownership than it was during the 1980s."

Even if millions of boomers stay put in their starter houses and remodel them into castles, millions more will probably move into bigger digs as their families and/or incomes grow. The bottom line is that more houses will become available at a time of smaller buster demand.

The buster advantage could well be heightened in the 1990s, as McArdle suggests, by bankers, homebuilders, and even the federal government lowering mortgage rates and improving tax incentives in an effort to spur construction and home investment, and thus the economy.

A growing segment of the first-time homebuyer market will be single busters, who naturally want smaller places than families, but something to call their own.

"My goal is to retire my student loans. Then I'd consider going out shopping for a place, or buying a place with a buddy, or something," says John McCarrick, 25, a second-year law student at Georgetown. "I know that renting is throwing money down the drain." Like many of his contemporaries, he's now living with his parents, "where the average rent is zero."

He hopes to be able to buy into a house by the time he's 28—two years into his law career. "I've discussed it with a couple of my friends, about getting a place, deciding in the long-run if we had the income and it was possible, definitely. You can share the costs, rather than rent." And going halvsies may be the only feasible way for a lot of young single busters to come up with a downpayment and mortgage.

173

"You don't want to throw the money away. You want to build up some equity," McCarrick reasons. That way, when a buster is finally ready to settle down and marry, "if you owned a place for six or seven years, you'd probably have enough equity for a downpayment on a 'family home' in the 'burbs, instead of a townhouse or condo."

While busters are indeed waiting longer to marry, a higher proportion of busters than previous generations may never marry. Various demographers suggest that something approaching 10 percent of busters may never marry, compared with the historic average of 5 percent.

"Speaking for the women, I can see many of us being single forever," says Jill Rogers, 26, who lives in suburban Chicago and works for the Fair Housing Center there. "But the majority of us see ourselves, say, by 35 or so buying our own little place and just going on."

In the meantime, she, like so many other busters, is living with her parents. I've been at home since day one. To me, I'm in a very comfortable situation. I don't really have a desire right now to do anything but still be at home. It's easier, moneywise," Rogers explains. "I pay $300 a month rent, which is just minimal. That's nothing compared to what a one-bedroom in Chicago would cost. You're looking there at $700, $800. So, why move?"

Down the road a few decades, busters with the money and the inclination will be in a good position to buy vacation and retirement spots—again because they will be buying primarily from boomers. Boomers are already investing in vacation homes, and the oldest among them is now just 18 years away from the traditional retirement age of 65, at which point some people begin to downsize again, vacating the larger homes in which they raised their families.

Because of the tremendous inventory of starter homes built for the baby boomers, Carliner expects that most busters will be buying existing, rather than new, homes. And while the busters who opened this chapter have hiked to the outer fringes of suburbia to find affordable dream homes, many of their contemporaries may not have to go so far.

"If you go back to World War II or so, younger people tended to move out to the fringes where there was less expensive housing," notes Carliner. "We may see less of that if we find that busters are buying existing homes. In that case, they will live closer to cities than if they were the market driving the construction."

Buster Biz

Opportunities for Buster Business

- **HAVE I GOT A DEAL FOR YOU.** Whatever busters want by way of shelter, somebody's got to sell it to them. Busters being busters, they'll want and expect a good price; so don't hold out for top dollar. They'll know they have the upper hand. Being fitness conscious, computer gherkins, and environmentally aware, they'll want a fitness room, a home office/computer command center, a Florida room, and maybe a greenhouse. The vast majority of the house-hunting buster couples will be career couples. They will have more to put down and more to buy what they want. Conveniences will be a top priority.

- **BUSTER BACHELOR PADS.** One in ten busters may never marry, double the historic rate of bachelorhood. These will be bachelors with a difference—they're busters, dude. They decorate in the buster style—Bart Simpson wallpaper, perhaps—and want the buster conveniences—health club, juice bars, and bike paths nearby. Expect their homes to be built from recycled materials. They're sure to give a shot in the arm to the market in smaller homes and condo conversions of efficiency apartments.

- **BUSTER BUDDIES.** Whether confirmed bachelors or just waiting longer to get married, there will be growing numbers of buster pals going into partnership to buy a house or condo as a way of combining resources to get into the real estate market and start building up equity. This is a way for young, underfinanced buyers to swing the downpayment and mortgage. Just as there are now roommate-finding services, there may emerge fee services that match up financially and personally compatible singles to pool funds to buy a house.

- **BOOMER BUYS.** There will be an oversupply of starter houses unloaded by boomers. A specialty may emerge for agents who search out scarce buster buyers of boomer homes. They'll serve as middlemen between generations the way others serve as liaisons between nations.

175

- **YOUR FRIENDLY BUSTER BANKER.** Okay, after some three decades of living with Mom and Pop, the busters have spotted their dream house and are ready to buy. But first, they'll need a mortgage. Bankers wanting to tap into this lucrative market can get leads by checking the files of their middle-aged customers. It's the grown offspring of these depositors who are still hanging around home. And when they're finally ready to flap away from the parental nest, they and their thankful parents will be looking for financing help. The parents are the entrée to the children, who will have some money saved up—possibly in your bank—from all those years spent at home.

· **WHAT ELSE HAVE YOU GOT?** One's nice, but two is twice as nice. Like every generation before them, upscale busters will want their own getaway spots. Some retirees are already beginning to bypass Florida in favor of out-of-the-way places in the Ozarks, Appalachia, the Carolinas, and other mountain and lake regions across the country. But busters will push out farther in those and other regions, to discover even less-traveled roads in their search for vacation retreats. Likely candidates will be in the outer reaches of collegetowns and state capitals, and wherever there's water or natural amenities. Sure, Florida's nice, but it's so crowded and expensive, and soon it will be filled with baby boomers—a guaranteed buster repellent.

CHAPTER FOURTEEN

Social Security

Increasing life expectancy and a senior boom dead-ahead add up to trouble for Social Security and busters, as well as boomers. The number of retirees drawing benefits is growing faster than the number of workers paying into the system. Things will get tense as boomers approach retirement age.

C armen Reschly, a baby buster born in 1966, is looking ahead and taking no chances. A bookkeeper at Texas Instruments in Dallas during the day, Reschly, who is single, works some nights as a cashier at Home Depot. "I really don't need it [two jobs] to survive. I need it more to pay off bills. I don't want any debt." She's also socking some money away into a retirement fund and going to college part-time in hopes of getting a promotion at Texas Instruments.

Motivating the hard-working Reschly are her doubts about Social Security. "We're not going to have enough money in the future. That's the way I'm looking at it," says Reschly, who worries that the massive baby-boom generation will overwhelm the federal retirement program. "I just know that I am not going to count on it."

A few miles from Dallas in the suburb of Irving, Texas, accountant Karen Meredith, who is a baby boomer, is also worried about the soundness of Social Security when it's time for her to retire. "I do tax returns for people my age, and every time we get to the Social Security taxes, the self-employment tax, I hear the same thing: 'Ha, ha, ha. You and I are never going to live to see a dime.' I said to one of my clients, 'Gee, I wish we had an AARP (American Association of Retired Persons) for us.' The client said, 'That's a great idea. You just have to do it.'"

177

So she did. In 1989, Karen Meredith formed the American Association of Boomers (AAB). Despite its name, Meredith says that the group's "objective has been to try to educate the public, the boomers and busters, seniors, whoever, that we do in fact have a problem. And we want to talk about it."

The organization already has 25,000 members in 50 states. Among the members is Carmen Reschly, who has volunteered her time to update the computerized membership files and handle mailings of the AAB's bimonthly newsletter, *My Generation*. Reschly explains her involvement this way: "It was something that I decided I wanted to do, because of the issue that Karen was trying to promote."

About 10 percent of the AAB's members are busters. Says Meredith: "Busters are joining because they see that our mission is to make sure that our huge numbers don't crush them. And they think that's a worthy cause."

If there's one thing that may finally bring boomers and busters together in a common cause, it's the looming mess known as Social Security. They will need one another to get the pension system finally fixed right so there's something left for them in the next century.

Then again, some observers foresee Social Security igniting generational wars, pitting boomers against busters, and maybe against their parents. Stay tuned.

The problem is quite simple. The number of Social Security recipients drawing benefits is growing much faster than the number of workers paying into the system. Things will start getting especially tense when boomers retire and the burden for supporting them falls to busters and the generations following them.

Contrary to logical assumptions, the money that the Social Security Administration withholds from a worker's paycheck is not going into an account to cover his or her future retirement. That would make sense and would work fine, but it's not what Franklin Roosevelt and Congress devised in 1935. Instead, the system taxes current workers to cover the benefits being paid out to current retirees.

When Social Security began paying out its first monthly benefits in 1940 (at $22.54 per month), there were 42 workers for each beneficiary. Intended as a supplement to other income rather than one's sole income in retirement, Social Security nevertheless expanded coverage and dramatically jumped payments over the decades. In 1956, coverage was expanded to include disabled workers as well as their families or survivors.

But by 1993, only 3.2 workers were paying into the system for each person now collecting benefits. By 2015, when the oldest baby boomers are settling into retirement, there will be only 2.7 workers supporting each beneficiary. By the time all boomers are retired and busters are ready to retire, there will be only 2 workers paying into the system for each retiree, according to Social Security's intermediate series of projections.

SOCIAL SECURITY: THE CONTRIBUTOR / RECIPIENT RATIO

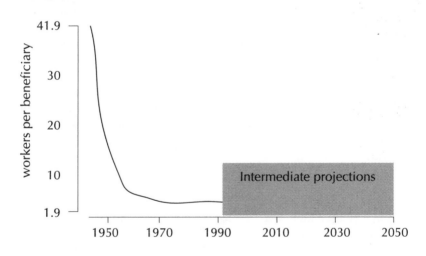

From a high of 41.9 workers contributing for every beneficiary in 1945, the ratio has plummeted to the current level of 3.4 contributors per beneficiary. By 2050, that number is projected to shrink to 1.9 contributors per beneficiary.

source: Social Security Administration

The inevitable crisis has been obscured by political posturing and the reassuringly huge but vulnerable surpluses currently in the two major Social Security trust funds. The assets of the Old-Age and Survivors Insurance Trust Funds and the Disability Insurance Trust Fund earned $19.8 billion in interest alone in fiscal 1991. Total Old-Age, Survivors and Disability Insurance (OASDI) assets reached $280.7 billion by January 1992. Those assets are projected to grow to $998 billion by 2001, or 206 percent of annual expenditures.

Sounds good. That's from pages 2 to 4 of the 1992 Annual Report of the Social Security's Board of Trustees. But read on—and closely. When looked at separately, the Disability Insurance Trust Fund's assets, which totaled $12.9 billion in 1992, are expected to be exhausted by 1997, according to Social Security's "most likely" intermediate projections.

The combined funds are in better shape for a few more decades, but only a few. OASDI tax revenues will be many times greater than expenditures for the next 24 years. This will cause a rapid accumulation of assets during that time, as will interest from the combined trust funds.

But boomers will be marching toward retirement and coming to collect. By 2024 and later, though, OASDI's total income will fall short of expenditures, according to Social Security's intermediate projections.

The trustees' report says, "In this circumstance, trust fund assets would be redeemed to cover the difference. The assets of the combined OASI and DI Trust Funds are estimated to be depleted under present law in 2036 based on intermediate assumptions." In 2036, half of baby boomers will still be in their 70s. The youngest buster, born in 1976, will be 60. And this comes after two major overhauls to prop up the system.

In 1977, Congress and Democratic President Jimmy Carter enacted a massive tax increase that proponents said would secure the system for "the rest of this century and well into the next," according to the 1978 OASDI Report. Time flies when you're having fun. By 1983, Congress and Republican President Ronald Reagan were at it again. This time, they insisted their fixes were permanent.

One of the fixes involves waiting longer to collect benefits. While those currently aged 55 and older can begin collecting full Social Security benefits at the traditional age of 65, the age is being pushed up one to two years for boomers and busters.

Better Start Saving

Current retirees and those about to retire—the parents of the boomers and busters—should do fine. Their timing is perfect. They'll likely collect full benefits, now averaging $653 a month for a retired worker and $1,106 for a retired couple who are both entitled to benefits. On the plus side, boomers and busters would appear to be well positioned at will-reading time to collect inheritance bonanzas from their folks. As trend tracker Ken Dychtwald, author of *Age Wave*, was quoted as saying in a 1991 article in *Nation's Business:* "People 65 and older own $3 trillion to $4 trillion in wealth and assets. Many are going to be passing on. And you'll see $3 trillion to $4 trillion in cars, insurance, stocks, and homes come cascading down to the boomers." No doubt, the forecast comforts countless boomers who have been notoriously slow to plan for their own retirements.

But now comes the bad news from *New Choices for Retirement Living* magazine, which reports that seniors are living it up and spending freely. In a national survey of 750 people aged 50 to 70, six in ten disagreed with the statement that "parents have an obligation to leave as much money as they can to their children to help them get a better start in life."

Seniors are also protecting their pensions, savings, and Social Security through membership in powerful lobbies like the Gray Panthers and the 18 million-member American Association of Retired Persons (AARP). Seniors also vote in very high proportions, a fact well-known to politicians who seek their support with vows that their benefits will not be touched.

The future financial problem for boomers and busters is compounded by their low savings rate, the shaky state of many private pension plans, and their typically low voter turnout.

181

A week into the presidency of the first baby-boomer president, Bill Clinton, the brokerage house of Merrill Lynch & Co. released a sobering report on Clinton's contemporaries, warning that they're saving only about one-third of what they need to live comfortably in retirement.

Princeton University economist B. Douglas Bernheim, who conducted the Merrill Lynch study, told the *Washington Post:* "Unless baby boomers become far more frugal, most will have to accept dramatically lower standards of living in retirement than they enjoyed during their working years."

Busters are still young and have time to save. But the boomers' inadequate savings rate will hurt not only themselves, but very possibly the busters who would be forced to support elderly boomers in the coming decades.

In the three presidential elections of the 1980s, less than 60 percent of people aged 25 to 44 bothered to vote, as did less than 40 percent of people under age 25, according to Census Bureau surveys. In contrast, more than two-thirds of people aged 45 to 64 and those aged 65 or older voted. Thus, seniors maximize their clout at the ballot box, while boomers and busters fail to use the strength that should come with their combined numbers. Turnout in the 1992 presidential election rose somewhat for all age groups. Still, older voters turned out in significantly higher proportions.

Interestingly, during the 1992 presidential campaign, the Republican and Democratic candidates danced around the radioactive issue of Social Security, obviously fearful of the wrath of senior voters. Third candidate Ross Perot was the most forceful in discussing the issue. In one of his half-hour campaign "infomercials," Perot called for increased taxes on Social Security payments going to upper-income recipients and cuts in cost-of-living raises to federal and military pensioners.

During the second televised campaign debate on October 15, 1992, in Richmond, Virginia, someone in the audience cited the Social Security Administration's projection of the insolvency of the trust fund by 2036. He proceeded to ask the candidates what they would do.

182

Then-President Bush contended: "The Social Security system was fixed about five years ago, and I think it's projected out to be sound beyond that. So at least we have time to work with it."

Perot, like the other candidates, spoke of the need to cut the deficit, but did not directly answer the question on Social Security that night.

Democratic candidate and future-president Bill Clinton spoke of the need to overhaul the health-care system and cut the budget. He danced around Social Security, saying, "By the time the century turns, we have got to have our deficit under control. We have to work it out so that surplus is building up so when the baby boomers like me retire, we're O.K."

Curiously, during a September 1, 1992, campaign speech in Macon, Georgia, Clinton, according to the *Washington Post,* asserted: "We don't need to tamper with Social Security ... We're not going to fool around with Social Security. It's solid. It's secure. It's sound. And I'm going to keep it that way."

Then he got elected. In his first televised State of the Union address, delivered before Congress on February 17, 1993, President Clinton spent an hour outlining a complex program of budget cuts and tax increases, aimed at trimming the swelling $4 trillion national debt.

On the matter of Social Security, there were no proposed cuts in benefits. However, Clinton asked Congress to approve an increase in taxes on Social Security benefits for recipients in upper-income brackets. If approved, 20 percent of beneficiaries, who now pay taxes on 50 percent of their Social Security benefits, would be liable for taxes on 85 percent of those benefits.

"The plan does ask older Americans with higher incomes who do not rely solely on Social Security to get by to contribute more," said Clinton. "This plan will not affect the 80 percent of Social Security recipients who do not pay taxes on Social Security now."

Needless to say, the proposal did not sit well with the AARP and millions of seniors. And while the Clinton Administration did gingerly take on a sacred cow, the proposal still does not address the underlying problems nor resolve the looming crisis of Social Security. But it is a start.

Early Warning Bell

Dorcas Hardy, Social Security commissioner under Ronald Reagan, has been trying to sound the alarm with her 1991 book *Social Insecurity: The Crisis in America's Social Security System and How to Plan Now for Your Own Financial Survival.* "When I became Commissioner of Social Security in 1986, I started out by stressing the financial integrity of the system and promised that the dollars would be there for everyone when they retired. But as I learned more about the future and watched Congress struggle to balance the budget, my enthusiasm became tempered. I began to limit the time span of my assurances to 'as long as you live' when the audience consisted primarily of those already receiving or about to receive benefits. When speaking to younger groups, I limited my promise to the year 2010 'or so.' And I tried to warn them that, in some circumstances, the crunch could come even earlier," she writes.

The crunch may come earlier if just a few of the more than a dozen economic and demographic assumptions used by the Social Security Administration to make its forecasts prove inaccurate. A protracted recession, high unemployment, rising life expectancy, and changes in immigration could bankrupt Social Security sooner rather than later. "The hard demographic and financial facts are that future retirees are unlikely, under any circumstances, to benefit as much from Social Security as their parents have," writes Hardy.

And worker taxes will probably go higher, much higher. When Social Security was created in 1935, its actuaries calculated that a combined payroll tax of 6 percent (half from the worker, half from the employer) was the most that would ever be needed to fund the system. "But the last time the payroll tax rate was 6 percent was during the Korean War, and it has been heading up ever since," reports *American Demographics* magazine in its February 1993 issue.

"The bottom line is that the combined payroll tax rate on covered workers now amounts to 12.4 percent for Social Security and 2.9 percent for Hospital Insurance (Medicare, Part A). Half of this, 7.7 percent, is what gets deducted on the FICA (Federal Insurance Contribution Act) line of your paycheck," the article continues.

"I have a retirement plan that I invest in on a monthly basis," says Jill Rogers, 26, who lives and works in suburban Chicago. Like many of her buster contemporaries, she isn't counting on Social Security. "You hear different things in the news and what have you about Social Security running out. I've heard rumors."

Rogers continues: "You look at somebody who's on Social Security now who has worked all their life. You wonder, 'Well, I'm just starting out. What's going to happen when I hit that age?' And you think about it. It's like 'wow!' But then you try not to think about it because you figure, 'Well, I'm only 26 years old and that's not going to happen.' Still you hear all the things on the media, and you can't help but wonder. I just kind of have the attitude, 'Well, we'll see.'"

Battle of the Ages

Dorcas Hardy warns of a possible war between the generations. "The baby boomers rebelled against their parents in the 1960s. Will they do it again in the 1990s? If they do, the battle will almost certainly be over Social Security—first taxes, then benefits."

• VOX BUSTER •

"One thing that concerns me is that you have a group of people who are relatively cohesive in the baby boom who are very used to voting. They're very, very aggressive. These people at one time thought they could change the world. I think they realize they can't do that now. But certainly, they're used to voting. And I think as they get older, they're going to tend more to vote for themselves as a bloc. ... I have a feeling that these people are going to change the rules, because they're used to the power, and what's the good of power if you're not going to use it."

—Robert Harvey, 28, Short Hills, New Jersey

The battle might go the other way—between boomers and busters who are fed up and not going to take it anymore. "With Social Security and Medicare straining under the burden of 60 to 70 million new retirees in 2016, the baby boomers may have no choice but to impose their will on younger Americans. However, if the baby boomers continue a life of self-indulgence, their children may decide to fight

185

back," according to Paul C. Light, a policy analyst and the author of the 1988 book *Baby Boomers.* "Programs like Social Security rely on a fragile social compact, not merely between kids and parents, but between parents and the future. If the baby boom invests nothing of itself in its own children's future, the compact will be severed. If that happens, an intergenerational war will come—not between the baby boom and its parents, but between the baby boom and its own children."

No doubt, there are going to be some battles and recriminations no matter what happens, but there is a third, less volatile way to proceed—build a coalition to gain sufficient support to fix the thing right once and for all.

"The sine qua non of any successful Social Security reform strategy must be an assurance to those already retired or nearing retirement that their benefits will be paid in full," write Stuart Butler and Peter Germanis in *Social Security: Prospects for Real Reform.* The 1985 book was an anthology of opinion by a dozen analysts, published by the Cato Institute, a Washington, D.C. think tank. "It was irresponsible in the first place for the federal government to promise unrealistic benefits. But it would be even more irresponsible now to break faith with the millions of people who have based their retirement plans on these expected benefits. Instead of spreading widespread panic among our elderly, which would only undermine our efforts to reform the system, we should acknowledge the system's liabilities as a total writeoff."

Having done that, Butler and Germanis see the need for a coalition of interest groups to face facts and reform the system thoroughly. "Building a constituency for Social Security reform requires mobilizing the various coalitions that stand to benefit from the change. Such a constituency is already extensive, but mobilizing it could become a self-generating process," they maintain.

The coalitions are already starting to form:

- Americans for Generational Equity (AGE) was launched in 1985 as a lobbying and information group in Washington, D.C., to represent the interests of young Americans—boomers and busters—in the Social Security debate and other issues that affect them. AGE produced research for legislators, media, employers, and interested citizens. While AGE is no longer active, it joined the battle, led the fight for over five years, and inspired others to support a worthy cause.

- The "Lead ... Or Leave" campaign, organized in 1992 by boomer Rob Nelson and buster Jon Cowan is calling on all members of Congress, the Senate, and the president to sign a pledge to attack the $4 trillion national debt. As a start, Lead ... Or Leave is pressing legislators to cut the annual budget deficit of $350 billion in half by 1996 or leave office. Not only are they pounding on the doors of Congress, but the group is also mounting a nationwide petition drive and a voter registration drive in cities across the U.S. and on over 50 college campuses.

- *The Next Progressive,* launched in 1991 as the first political and opinion magazine of, by, and for busters, has emerged as a quarterly bully pulpit for twentysomethings with complaints, creative ideas, and possible solutions on Social Security and other challenges their generation faces.

- The American Association of Boomers (AAB) continues to make waves on Social Security. In addition to those who joined the AAB on their own, some busters and boomers have been enrolled by their retired parents, who are concerned for their children's future. AAB is raising tough issues and getting people thinking through its bimonthly newsletter, media interviews, and a speakers' bureau.

The debate is sure to get noisier, as boomers and busters get worked up. Remember that boomers, who cut their political teeth on the anti-war protests of the 1960s, know how to be heard and to get what they want. With busters at their side, they will be pressing politicians from the local to the national level and running for office themselves on platforms that call for the sound overhaul of Social Security.

The potential for coalitions between boomers and busters can be glimpsed in the successful 1992 presidential campaign of Bill Clinton, who made a concerted effort to woo busters by talking up their concerns about jobs, the economy, and health care.

Boomers and busters will eventually be working from within the ranks of the AARP. The oldest boomers are only three years away from eligibility at age 50. Facing up to shifting demographics, AARP is already beginning to change its tune. A revealing ad that ran in the national newspaper supplement *Parade* in September 1992 showed a smiling baby girl in bib overalls beneath the headline, "We're already planning for her retirement."

The copy read: "The issues she'll have to face in the 21st century must be dealt with now. That's why we're already looking at how America's changing economy, the health care crisis, and the future of Social Security will affect her financial prospects and retirement options. We're AARP. And while we're committed to making life better for everyone age 50 and over today, we're just as concerned about anyone who'll be 50 and over later. Even much later."

• VOX BUSTER •

"I think everybody kind of needs to get together and say, 'Hey, you know: this is wrong, this is wrong, this is wrong.' We all need to work together, because we're all here. You know, not that the younger generation needs to take over, or you guys need to take over, the older generation. It's just that everybody needs to work together."

—Jim McFadden, 28, Moreno Valley, California

What form the Social Security overhaul should and will take is a matter of debate. Many proposals have already been advanced from various quarters. Dorcas Hardy presents several major ones.

Hardy's own recommendations include balancing the federal budget, using current Social Security surpluses for future retirees, raising the age of entitlement to 70 by the year 2020 or so, eliminating penalties for current recipients who also work, and encouraging people to save and invest in private pensions.

Many others who have studied Social Security also see the need to further raise the age of entitlements and to lighten the burden on Social Security by getting people to save and invest more in private pension plans and insurance policies. That could be done with tax incentives. In 1974, Congress created Individual Retirement Accounts (IRAs), which allowed people to deposit $10,000 annually in a nontaxable interest-bearing account. They became so popular that the government began worrying about loss of tax revenues. In 1986, Congress rewrote the tax laws yet again and cut tax incentives for buying IRAs.

Seeing an opportunity, Merrill Lynch created its Fund for Tomorrow in 1984, a portfolio of stocks aimed at first-time (baby-boom) investors. The fund has grown from $51 million in assets to its current level of over $500 million. Prudential has also begun focusing on nervous boomers, who are belatedly awakening to their financial responsibilities in the coming decades. The marketing strategy has been expanded to include the newest young investors—busters. If boomers are starting to plan for the 21st century now, busters can't be far behind.

Fidelity Investments, which has advertised on television with a toll-free number for retirement planning information, sends callers a fat package on IRAs, mutual funds, stocks, and CDs. So that no one misses the point about who should be preparing for the future, one brochure carries a color cover photo of a picnicking couple, clearly baby boomers, surrounded by their two little children and two elderly parents.

"Today people are taking better care of themselves and living longer, which obviously means longer retirements, too. And you probably will want to maintain an active lifestyle after you retire, rather than worrying about whether your finances will last," the brochure begins.

The next page cautions: "For most of us, Social Security and company pension benefits will not provide the level of income required to maintain the same standard of living in retirement that we have in our working years. ...The key to effective retirement planning is making the most of the time you have until retirement. That means starting now and saving regularly."

The two-year-old Gulf Atlantic Life Insurance Company, the first Hispanic-owned and -operated life insurance company, is even taking aim at Hispanics looking toward the future. While insurance is pretty much insurance, Gulf Atlantic believes it has the advantage in the Hispanic community, because its salespeople are bilingual and ads are specifically crafted to that target audience.

The Sunshine State, America's Laboratory

For a glimpse of what the U.S. might be like when boomers hit retirement age and how busters and the rest of society might care for them, one should look at Florida now. Here's why: over 18 percent of Florida's residents are aged 65 or older. One in five Floridians is a senior. That's the proportion that the U.S. will hit around the year 2020, when the first half of the baby boom has reached its 65th birthday.

Trend tracker John Naisbitt has called Florida a bellwether state. In his 1982 bestseller, *Megatrends,* Naisbitt says: "By carefully watching what is happening now in Florida, we stand to learn a wealth of information about the problems and opportunities the whole nation will face in the future."

Of Florida's 2.5 million senior residents, 80 percent are fully independent. "Only 2 percent of Florida's senior citizens are confined to nursing homes, largely because of our recent successes in providing home and community care," notes the 1987 state report *Keys to Florida's Future: Winning In a Competitive World.* Realizing that active, independent seniors are happier, productive, and not a drain on society, Florida already has numerous strategies in place to keep seniors self-sufficient as long as possible, thus lightening the burden on the state, its other residents, and the health-care system.

Here are just a few of the creative things being done in Florida to meet the senior challenge:

• The state Department of Elder Affairs recruits volunteers for "respite care" to care for infirm seniors for a few hours, thus giving a spouse a break. Retired doctors, nurses, computer experts, and others are also sought as volunteers to put their talents to work helping shut-ins. And small stipends are available to active seniors who visit and do light chores for shut-ins, thus helping out all parties.

• Developers and apartment managers are promoting "independent living" apartments and condos, where residents have their own private units but take meals in a common dining room. Medical care is available on site, and there is van service to nearby shopping. Meanwhile, nonprofit groups are promoting the share-a-home concept, teaming up small groups of seniors not only to share the cost and chores in renting a house, but also to provide one another with companionship.

• Businesses are encouraged and eager to hire seniors as part-time workers, because they're experienced and highly productive, with low absenteeism. Malls and fast-food restaurants are filled with clerks, managers, and security guards who are well past age 65. These jobs provide seniors with extra money, activity, and friends. At the same time, employers like Southern Bell give workers time off from the job to do volunteer work with senior citizens.

Busters, take note. For your own financial solvency, reread the three previous paragraphs and start brainstorming on other strategies. A big part of the solution to America's looming Social Security/pension mess is for busters and everybody else to keep boomers healthy, active, working, and financially independent as long as possible, and thus less dependent on Social Security.

Buster Biz

Opportunities for Buster Business

- **TIME OUT.** Retirement is still more than three full decades away for busters. But they—and their financial advisers—better start preparing now and not count on Social Security. That's where bankers, accountants, insurance agents, and financial advisers come into the picture. The time to start planning for the golden years is now, so they don't tarnish.

- **SOCIAL SECURITY WATCH.** With each passing year, the Social Security system comes closer to exhausting its reserves, and pressure mounts to quit the political pandering and find real solutions. No matter what the source, if the talk is straight and the strategies sound, buster ears will listen.

- **SENIOR SERVICES.** When boomers retire, busters and everybody else will need cost-effective strategies to meet seniors' demands for goods and services, in ways that do not disrupt the rest of society. It can no longer be business as usual for volunteer and for-profit organizations when it comes to senior services. Look to Florida.

- **DON'T STOP NOW.** Boomers and busters alike will be working longer than did their parents as a way of easing the Social Security crunch. Career counselors and job-placement specialists will be needed to best match boomer and buster talent and preferences to the job needs of the 21st century.

- **ON THE MOVE.** To make their nest eggs go further, many boomers and then busters will eventually sell their suburban dream homes to buy smaller, less costly places in the countryside, where the living is easy and a lot cheaper.

CHAPTER FIFTEEN

The Verdict ... So Far

Busters are quietly taking up their places in the real world. They're your new colleagues at work, the new crop of doctors, the young police officers you pass on the street, the entrepreneurs coming up with the latest hot ventures. A buster may one day be your boss.

Undeterred U.S. and Coalition forces, under the leadership of General H. Norman Schwarzkopf, were victorious in the 43-day 1991 Desert Storm war with Iraq. Some 541,000 American troops served in that war; their average age was 20.5.

It is estimated that over one-quarter of America's police and firefighters who battle crime and fires daily to protect all of us are in their 20s.

In 1992, underrated Jennifer Capriati defeated heavy favorite Steffi Graf to win the Olympic women's singles tennis title. Spunky Capriati, a 16-year-old high schooler from Florida, was the youngest woman ever to win the gold medal.

In the National Football League, where the average salary for the 1992–93 season was a not-too-shabby $505,000, the average age of players was 26, which makes most of them a few years younger than the first Ford Mustangs.

193

Shaquille O'Neal, the basketball phenomenon from Louisiana State University, signed the fattest NBA contract ever, $40 million over seven years, with the expansion team the Orlando Magic. The overnight multi-millionaire will have many years to enjoy his newfound wealth. He was only 20 when he signed his contract in 1992.

In 1993, the medical schools of America will graduate 15,000 new physicians, most of whom will be about 26 years old and one-third of whom will be women. Among them will be many who will go into the burgeoning geriatic specialty. One of them may find a cure for cancer or AIDS.

Daryl Bernstein, who has launched some 50 businesses during his varied career, is also the author of *Better Than a Lemonade Stand: Small Business Ideas for Kids.* "He completed his book in four months by getting up every morning at 3 and writing until it was time for school. He got the book to his publisher in time to be heralded as the youngest author signing books at the 1992 American Booksellers Association convention," reported the *Wall Street Journal.* He was 16 years old at the time.

These young success stories are all busters, including college-dropout Michael Dell, who landed on *Forbes* magazine's 1992 list of the 400 richest Americans. "As a teenager, ran stamp and coin auctions on weekends, sold newspaper subscriptions to targeted audience, new-lyweds. Sold hard-drive kits for IBM-PC out of dorm room. Dropped out freshman year, launched own company at age 19. Transformed selling, servicing, pricing of IBM-compatibles: handled by phone, catalogs at cut-rate prices. Hired engineers to build inexpensive IBM clones," reported the October 19, 1992, issue of *Forbes.* His esti-mated worth—$310 million.

A few weeks earlier, *Forbes* released its list of "The Top 40" entertain-ers for 1992. Ranked fourth among them are New Kids on the Block, busters who pull down over $50 million a year...Then there's 28-year-old Jon Cowan, half of the "Lead ...Or Leave" campaign, which may just help cut the federal deficit and salvage Social Security for all Americans.

The director of the NAACP's West Coast region is Shannon Reeves, a civil rights activist and rising leader in the African-American community. At age 24, he is the youngest person to hold an NAACP regional directorship. His major goals are to attract a new generation of African Americans to active membership in the NAACP and to encourage financial investment in the African-American community and patronage of black businesses.

While Bill Clinton is the first baby boomer to occupy the White House, baby buster and reporter Tabitha Soren helped put him there with her up-close coverage that introduced the candidate to many new voters. For anybody over age 30 who doesn't know this now-famous journalist, the 25-year-old Soren is MTV's hard-hitting political reporter, who went on to interview and profile all the major presidential candidates for her buster viewers. In so doing, she may have emerged as the most influential reporter of the 1992 presidential campaign, eclipsing the aging, million-dollar anchors Dan Rather, Tom Brokaw, and Peter Jennings.

Baldwin Park, California, a Los Angeles suburb with a population of 70,000 and a $25 million annual budget, has a new and unusual mayor in Fidel Vargas. "I am not a politician. I am a public servant," Vargas recently wrote in *The Next Progressive*. He's 24, the youngest mayor in America. "I had the ideas, the vision, and the power to create positive change."

Going to the mound for the New York Yankees in the 1993 season is 26-year-old pitcher Jim Abbott, arguably the big leaguer with the most perseverance and heart around the majors. An inspiration to all, he was born without a right hand, yet clearly overcame that handicap.

You get the point. Busters are arriving quietly and slowly, but steadily, surprising many of their elders. Unlike boomers who noisily blast along every step of the way, busters have come from obscurity and are beginning to take their rightful place.

• VOX BUSTER •

"I don't think we'll be drowned out. People get into positions of authority and after a while, the tide turns and the old people are out and new people are in. I really don't see that the size of our generation is going to have a big impact on that. The bottom line is: people aren't going to be doing the same thing forever. There's going to be a bit less new blood in circulation and new people in different places. So, our time will come."

195

—Barry Shook, 28
Born January 5, 1965—one of America's first baby busters

While misconceptions and ignorance about busters abound, their early achievements are sure to impress all but chronic skeptics and myopic media pundits. Buster accomplishments should prompt reappraisal among many.

Given the choice between a highly touted generation, like the baby boom, or an underrated and misunderstood group like the busters, the advantage and the ultimate victory may go to the busters. They have the elements of surprise and mystery about them, a feistiness and lone-wolf determination that will serve them well, qualities that come from having to assert themselves to be heard above the boomer din, and lower expectations that they are sure to surpass by a wide margin. Take heart, busters, and find encouragement from those emerging among you. As for the rest of us, let's start to watch and listen to them closely. We have much to learn; they have much to teach us. They are the future. And after all, ultimately we're all on the same side.

A Boomer's Buster Forecast, and Other Final Thoughts

- The first buster, just a few years past age 30, will be elected to Congress in the year 2000—at the dawn of the 21st century. Crucial to the victory will be the support of the buster bloc, which began flexing its muscles in the presidential election of 1992. More unified than other groups, the buster voters will respond to candidates hitting the hot buster button issues—environment, equity, and getting their voice heard in Washington. Taking a cue from Uncle Bill Clinton, the first president to take busters seriously, the first buster in Congress will campaign heavily on MTV and win the endorsement of that unorthodox yet influential rock network.

- Busters are growing—not only in clout, but in numbers. No, there aren't more baby busters being born. But immigration has already added 3 million busters to the 41 million who were born in the U.S. By 2015, busters could total 47 million, according to the latest Census Bureau projections. Newcomers will share with native-born busters the concern for Social Security and the growing burden of supporting boomers in their retirement. Other common issues among newcomers and homegrown busters: job advancement, schooling, and housing opportunities.

- A combat veteran of Desert Storm will likely be the first buster elected president, possibly as early as the election of 2012. She will be neither a Republican nor a Democrat, but rather from the fledgling GOP, the

197

Guarantor of Pensions Party, which will form sometime during the 1990s to salvage Social Security.

- More racially and ethnically diverse than older generations, busters hold the key to improving race relations in America. Others talk and worry about those relations, often from within their own enclave. But busters have experienced more diversity and a greater degree of integration—in the classroom, the workplace, the gym, and the neighborhood. That's not without tension and collisions. Still, busters of all colors know one another well and talk to each other. Their elders may have something to learn from them on getting along.

- In another five or ten years, most busters will have decamped from their rooms in their parents' homes. Most will eventually marry and become parents. They will tell their children how tough it was growing up and how they are going to make it better for their kids. Busters will strive for the stability in their families that so many of them didn't have when they were young. They'll probably be conscientious and spend more time with their children than they got to spend with their own parents. Slower to marry and slower to divorce, busters will cause the U.S. to relinquish its dubious distinction of being the "divorcingest" nation in the world.

- On the other hand, some 4 million busters will never marry at all—about one in ten. Bachelor busters will emerge as the hot niche market of the late 1990s. Approaching their years of peak earning and consumption, they're primed to spend lots of money on themselves.

- Harried workers, hang on. Busters and robots will make sure that the work week, which used to average over 40 hours, will be plunging toward the low 30s. Skill mismatch, labor shortages in some sectors, and independent busters refusing to work past quitting time will prompt employers to trim the work week to keep busters content.

- Many busters, primarily those in their later years, will work from home, especially those who developed a facility with computers during their school years. Instead of commuting by car to work, busters increasingly will commute by computer, instantaneously transmitting their work from home to the office with the push of a button.

- You have no doubt heard of AARP and the Gray Panthers, those pressure groups for seniors. They're bound to face competition from a group calling itself AAWB, the American Association of Working Busters. The AAWB will fight the battles over equity and pensions that need to be fought for busters. The seeds for such an organization are already being sown by groups like Lead ... Or Leave and the twenty-something magazine, *The Next Progressive.*

- The first busters reach age 65 in the year 2030. But they and the busters following them won't be retiring at that age, or anytime close to it. While the Social Security Administration hiked the age of buster eligibility for full benefits to 67 in 1983, it will likely push the age requirement back a few more years yet again. Busters can probably expect to work until age 70, but at least they won't be slaving for the 40 hours a week like their parents and grandparents did.

- Diversity, a hot issue in the 1980s and early 1990s, promotes inclusion of more people from underrepresented groups in our universities, the news media, advertising, and the corporate world. The focus has been almost exclusively on racial and ethnic minorities, as well as women, with class-action lawsuits being filed when their numbers don't match their proportions in the population. A new minority will be added to the diversity debate of the 1990s and beyond—busters.

- The once-massive baby-boom generation will eventually begin shrinking, as actuarial tables and past bad habits catch up with them. Sometime between 2035 and 2040, according to the latest Census Bureau projections, busters will actually outnumber boomers. Finally! By then, the youngster buster will be 64; the oldest boomer, 94. But long before that, busters will overtake boomers in cultural and corporate clout as boomers settle into retirement and eventually shift from go-go to slow-go and then no-go status. In another 20 or 30 years, busters will be running a lot of America—corporations, the military, networks, newspapers. Radio stations will then shift programming formats yet again, playing golden oldies from the 1980s and 1990s, featuring classic rock by Pearl Jam, Red Hot Chili Peppers, Luther Vandross, Metallica, Run DMC, Jane's Addiction, and Nirvana.

Battle of the Tape: Busters vs. Boomers

	Busters	Boomers
Current size	44 million	78 million
Birthdates	1965-76	1946-64
Share of U.S. population	17 percent	30 percent
Influential toy	Nintendo	Hula hoop
Favorite TV shows	Seinfeld; Star Trek: The Next Generation; In Living Color; 20/20; Arsenio Hall	Laugh-In; Star Trek; Saturday Night Live; 60 Minutes; The Tonight Show
Favorite comic	Calvin & Hobbes	Doonesbury
Favorite cartoon	The Simpsons; Ren & Stimpy	Rocky & Bullwinkle
Music of youth	R&b; industrial dance music; hip hop; grunge (Seattle sound)	Rock; r&b; disco; country
Musical medium	MTV; FM; Underground clubs	FM; soft-rock; oldies Woodstock
Defining music group	Nirvana; Run DMC; Pearl Jam	Beatles; Stones; Elvis; Led Zeppelin
Preferred reading	*Spin*	*Rolling Stone*

	Busters	**Boomers**
SAT scores (average combined)	1990: 900	1965: 969
Preferred college majors	Business; computer science	English literature; psychology; sociology
Time needed to graduate	5.8 years	4.5 years
War	Desert Storm	Vietnam
Majority position	Support war	Oppose war
First political involvement	Collecting for Public Interest Research Group to fight polluters	Massive protests to stop a war
Novel	*Generation X*	*Catcher in the Rye*
Defining moments	Exxon Valdez Oil spill; Tiananmen Square crackdown; 1990 recession	Kennedy/King assassinations; Wall Street crash, 1987
Scandal	S&L mess	Watergate
Preferred greeting	Hey, dude!	Peace!
Preferred superlative	Awesome	Groovy
Drug of choice	Imported beer	Marijuana

	Busters	Boomers
Complaint of choice	You're destroying the ozone layer.	What about my feelings?
First multi-millionaires	Michael Dell; Shaquille O'Neal	Donald Trump; Steven Jobs
Biggest fear	Supporting boomers in their old age	Getting old
Biggest hopes	Boomers get out of the way; Someday we'll run things...	Aging cure found; We run things until we're finally ready to escape to the woods, mountains, or shore for peace and quiet for everybody...

Appendices

••••

Suggested Sources

- *Advertising Age*
- American Association of Boomers, Irving, TX
- *American Demographics,* Ithaca, NY
- Bureau of Labor Statistics, Washington, DC
- Census Bureau, Washington, DC
- *Details*
- *Entertainment Weekly*
- Fox Network
- Lead ... Or Leave, Washington, DC
- *Mademoiselle*
- MTV
- National Association for the Advancement of Time Los Angeles, CA
- National Center for Education Statistics, Washington, DC
- *The Numbers News,* Ithaca, NY
- Popular Culture Department, Bowling Green State University, Bowling Green, OH
- Population Reference Bureau, Washington, DC
- *Sassy*
- *Slacker*—movie and book
- Social Security Administration, Washington, DC
- Teenage Research Unlimited, Northbrook, IL
- *The New York Times*
- *The Next Progressive*
- *USA Today*
- *The Wall Street Journal*

Bibliography

Articles

Bernstein, Aaron, et al. "What Happened to the American Dream?" *Business Week*, New York, NY, August 19, 1991.

Blumenfeld, Laura. "The Goo-Goo Crew: These Kids Suck on Pacifiers and Dance With Dolls. Regression Is the Latest Rage." *Washington Post*, Washington, DC, December 17, 1992.

Borrell, Jerry, et al. "America's Shame: The Creation of the Technological Underclass in America's Public Schools—How We Abandoned Our Children's Future." *Macworld*, San Francisco, CA, September 1992.

Dear Dr. Demo, "Social Insecurity." *American Demographics,* Ithaca, NY, February 1993.

Deutschman, Alan. "What 25-Year-Olds Want." *Fortune,* New York, NY, August 27, 1990.

Deutschman, Alan. "The Upbeat Generation." *Fortune*, New York, NY, July 13, 1992.

Dunn, William. "Hanging Out With American Youth." *American Demographics*, Ithaca, NY, February 1992.

Dunn, William. "The Move Toward Ethnic Marketing." *Nation's Business,* Washington, DC, July 1992.

205

Mankiw, N. Gregory and David N. Weil "The Baby Boom, the Baby Bust, and the Housing Market." *Regional Science and Urban Economics* 19, Elsevier Science Publishers, 1989.

Riche, Martha Farnsworth. "The Boomerang Age." *American Demographics,* Ithaca, NY, May 1990.

Zinn, Laura, et al. "Move Over Boomers: The Busters are Here—And They're Angry." *Business Week,* New York, NY, December 14, 1992.

Books

Celente, Gerald, with Tom Milton. *Trend Tracking,* Warner Books, New York, NY, 1990.

Coupland, Douglas. *Generation X,* St. Martin's Press, New York, NY, 1991.

Dunn, William. *Selling the Story: The Layman's Guide to Collecting and Communicating Demographic Information,* American Demographics Books, Ithaca, NY, 1992.

Easterlin, Richard A. *Birth and Fortune: The Impact of Numbers on Personal Welfare.* 2nd edition, University of Chicago Press, Chicago, IL, 1987.

Ferrara, Peter J., ed. *Social Security: Prospects for Real Reform,* Cato Institute, Washington, DC, 1985.

Forester, Tom. *High-Tech Society,* The MIT Press, Cambridge, MA, 1987.

Fosler, R. Scott, et al. *Demographic Change and the American Future.* University of Pittsburgh Press, Pittsburgh, PA, 1990.

Graham, Lawrence and Lawrence Hamdan. *Youthtrends: Capturing the $200 Billion Youth Market,* St. Martin's Press, New York, NY, 1987.

Hardy, Dorcas R. and C. Colburn Hardy. *Social Insecurity: The Crisis in America's Social Security System and How to Plan Now for Your Own Financial Survival,* Villard Books, New York, NY, 1991.

Johnson, Otto, et al. *Information Please Almanac 1993,* Houghton Mifflin Company, Boston, MA, 1992.

Kowinski, William Severini. *The Malling of America,* William Morrow & Company, New York, NY, 1985.

Lichter, S. Robert, Linda S. Lichter, and Stanley Rothman. *Watching America,* Prentice Hall Press, New York, NY, 1991.

Light, Paul C. *Baby Boomers,* W.W. Norton & Company, New York, NY, 1988.

McNeal, James U. *Kids As Customers: A Handbook of Marketing to Children,* Lexington Books, New York, NY, 1992.

Naisbitt, John and Patricia Aburdene. *Megatrends 2000,* William Morrow & Company, New York, NY, 1990.

Russell, Cheryl. *100 Predictions for the Baby Boom: The Next 50 Years,* Plenum Publishing Corporation, New York, NY, 1987.

Journals

Gallup, George. *Gallup Poll Monthly,* George Gallup Organization, Princeton, NJ.

Klein, Deborah P., ed., *Monthly Labor Review,* Bureau of Labor Statistics, Washington, DC, November 1991.

Monographs

Bianchi, Suzanne M. *America's Children: Mixed Prospects,* Population Reference Bureau, Washington, DC, 1990.

De Vita, Carol J. *America in the 21st Century: A Demographic Overview,* Population Reference Bureau, Washington, DC, 1989.

Trout, Peggy S. *Fast Facts & Figures About Social Security,* Social Security Administration, Washington, DC, 1990.

Reports

Alsalam, Nabeel, Laurence T. Ogle, Gayle Thompson Rogers, and Thomas M. Smith. *The Condition of Education 1992.* National Center for Education Statistics, Washington, DC, 1992.

Brady, Nicholas F., et al. 1992 *Annual Report of the Board of Trustees of the Federal Old-Age and Survivors Insurance and the Federal Disability Insurance Trust Funds,* Social Security Administration, Washington, DC, 1992.

Callis, Robert R. *Homeownership Trends in the 1980s,* U.S. Bureau of the Census, Washington, DC, 1990.

Day, Jennifer Cheeseman. *Population Projections of the United States, by Age, Sex, Race, and Hispanic Origin: 1992 to 2050,* U.S. Bureau of the Census, Washington, DC, 1992.

DeAre, Diana. *Geographical Mobility: March 1990 to March 1991,* U.S. Bureau of the Census, Washington, DC, 1992.

Elliott, Emerson J. *Digest of Education Statistics, 1992.* National Center for Education Statistics, Washington, DC, 1992.

Foertsch, Mary A. *Reading In and Out of School,* National Center for Education Statistics, Washington, DC, 1992.

Grier, George. *The Baby Bust,* The Washington Center for Metropolitan Studies, Washington, DC, 1971.

Jacobs, John E. *The State of Black America, 1993,* The National Urban League, New York, NY, 1993.

Jennings, Jerry T. *Voting and Registration in the Election of November 1990,* U.S. Bureau of the Census, Washington, DC, 1991.

Jennings, Jerry T. *Voting and Registration in the Election of November 1992,* U.S. Bureau of the Census, Washington, DC, to be published late 1993.

Joint Center for Housing Studies of Harvard University. *The State of the Nation's Housing 1992,* Joint Center for Housing Studies of Harvard University, Cambridge, MA, 1991.

Kominski, Robert. *Computer Use in the United States: 1989,* U.S. Bureau of the Census, Washington, DC, 1991.

Labor, U.S. Department of. *Consumer Expenditures in 1991,* Bureau of Labor Statistics, Washington, DC, December 1992.

Lino, Mark. *Expenditures on a Child by Families, 1991,* U.S. Department of Agriculture, Family Economics Research Group, Washington, DC, 1992.

Rawlings, Steve W. *Household and Family Characteristics: March 1991,* U.S. Bureau of the Census, Washington, DC, 1992.

Saluter, Arlene F. *Marital Status and Living Arrangements: March 1992,* U.S. Bureau of the Census, Washington, DC, 1992.

Silverman, Mark, et al. *News 2000,* Gannett Corporation, Rosslyn, VA, 1992.

Surveys

Astin, A. W., E.L. Dey, W.S. Korn, and E.R. Riggs. *The American Freshman: National Norms for Fall 1991,* Higher Education Research Institute, University of California, Los Angeles, CA, 1991.

Charlton Research, Inc., and Hamilton and Staff. "The 1992 MTV News Political Poll," Charlton Research, Inc., San Francisco, CA, and Hamilton and Staff, Washington, DC, July 1992.

Dey, E. L., A.W. Astin, and W.S. Korn. *The American Freshman: Twenty-five Year Trends,* Higher Education Research Institute/University of California, Los Angeles, CA, 1991.

Guccione, Bob Jr. "Campus Survey," *Spin,* New York, NY, March 1992.

Guccione, Bob Jr. "Readers Poll," *Spin,* New York, NY, June 1992.

Hart, Peter D. "MTV/Rock the Vote National Youth Survey," Peter D. Hart Research Associates, Washington, DC, July 1992.

Himmelfarb, Stuart, et al. Roper CollegeTrack, The Roper Organization, New York, NY, annual.

Josephson, Michael. "Ethical Values, Attitudes and Behaviors in American Schools-1992," The Joseph and Edna Josephson Institute of Ethics, Marina del Rey, CA, 1992.

Roper Organization. "Twentysomething: The New Individual," The Roper Organization, New York, NY, May 1992.

Setlow, Carolyn E., Ronald Bass, and Connie J. Schroyer. "Analysis of the 1990 Survey of High School Youth and Parents," Harris/Scholastic Research, New York, NY, 1990.

Audio Tapes

Crispell, Diane, et al. "The Post-Boomers: A New Breed," Consumer Outlook XI, American Demographics, Ithaca, NY, 1991.

Index

* indicates table or chart

Photo by Christine Dunn

William Dunn is a contributing editor of *American Demographics®* magazine, a Dow Jones monthly business magazine. He is the author of *Selling The Story: The Layman's Guide to Collecting and Communicating Demographic Information.* His reports on demographic trends have also appeared in *Nation's Business.*

He began writing about demographics in 1977 at *The Detroit News,* one of the first reporters in the country to cover population trends as a regular beat. From 1986 to 1990, he was the demographics writer for *USA Today* and the Gannett News Service.

Mr. Dunn's articles on a variety of other topics have been published in numerous major publications, including *The New York Times, The New York Daily News, The Los Angeles Times, The Boston Globe, Us, Publishers Weekly,* and *Writer's Digest.*

Mr. Dunn lives in Chevy Chase, Maryland with his wife Christine, and is currently working on another book on demographics, as well as a history of the golden age of American cartooning.

TARGETING FAMILIES:
Marketing To and Through the New Family
Word-of-mouth product recommendations made from one family member to another are significantly more effective than those made between friends or colleagues. Learn how to get family members on your sales force and how to implement a "Full Family Marketing" approach that attracts youths, spouses, and seniors.

CAPTURING CUSTOMERS:
How to Target the Hottest Markets of the '90s
Find out how to use consumer information to identify opportunities in nearly every market niche.

BEYOND MIND GAMES:
The Marketing Power of Psychographics
The first book that details what psychographics is, where it came from, and how you can use it.

SELLING THE STORY:
The Layman's Guide to Collecting and Communicating Demographic Information
A handbook offering a crash course in demography and solid instruction in writing about numbers. Learn how to use numbers carefully, how to avoid misusing them, and how to bring cold numbers to life by relating them to real people.

THE SEASONS OF BUSINESS:
The Marketer's Guide to Consumer Behavior
Learn which demographic groups are the principle players and which consumer concerns are most pressing in each marketing season.

DESKTOP MARKETING:
Lessons from America's Best
Dozens of case studies show you how top corporations in all types of industries use today's technology to find tomorrow's customers.

The Insider's Guide to Demographic Know-How: How to Find, Analyze, and Use Information About Your Customers
A comprehensive directory, explaining where to find the data you need, often at little or no cost. Now in its third edition.

Health Care Consumers in the 1990s: A Handbook of Trends, Techniques, and Information Sources for Health Care Executives
This handbook makes the connection between demographic realities and related health care issues. It will help you define your target market and carve out a niche that you can serve profitably and effectively.

ALSO FROM AMERICAN DEMOGRAPHICS

American Demographics magazine is your guide to understanding today's consumer marketplace. It does more than report on the trends; it provides unique insights on your customers and prospects. Annual subscription $62

The Numbers News is a monthly newsletter about the trends defining U.S. consumer markets in the 1990s and beyond. As the population becomes increasingly diverse, you need the most up-to-date information available about demographics and consumer trends. To stay ahead of your competition, you need it first. Annual subscription $149

Marketing Tools Catalog is an all-inclusive source of books, topical reprint packages, slides, audio cassettes, speech transcripts, software, and other products for marketing and planning professionals. Request your free copy today!

For more information about American Demographics publications, contact our Customer Service Center at 800-828-1133 or write to American Demographics, P.O. Box 68, Ithaca, New York, 14851

AMERICAN DEMOGRAPHICS INC.
A DOW JONES COMPANY